James

May all of your mountains prove ever easier to ?

Glenn D. O'Hallaron...

May '96

MOUNTAINS OUT OF MOLEHILLS

By the same author

You Sign

2nd Edition 1992

British Library Cataloguing in Publication Data
O'Halloran, Terence P.
Mountains out of Molehills — 1st Ed.
I. Title
ISBN 1 85609 048 5

MOUNTAINS OUT OF MOLEHILLS

by

Terence P O'Halloran
B.Sc., A.C.I.I., F.L.I.A. (dip).

LONDON
WITHERBY & CO. LTD
32-36 Aylesbury Street,
London EC1R 0ET

1st EDITION 1993

MONUMENT
SERIES

© Terence P O'Halloran
1993

ISBN 1 85609 048 5

Printed and Published by
Witherby & Co. Ltd.
32-36 Aylesbury Street
London EC1R 0ET

Tel No: 071 251 5341
Fax No: 071 251 1296

PREFACE

This is not a book of ideas. This is a book containing work methods that have been used time and time again to secure 350 plus cases every year for the last twenty years, by Terence O'Halloran.

Most of the ideas are not original. They are amplifications or variations of one page presentations put together by a multiplicity of successful life assurance sales people.

Terence O'Halloran is a professional buyer. Ask any organisation who the most important member of their team is. It is the buyer.

"Buyers" know their market place, product range, price tolerances and they negotiate on behalf of their "employer". Our employer is inevitably the client.

There are many "well it worked once for me, it must be a good sales idea" one pagers around. The advantage of using the contents of this book, is that it is a blow by blow account of how a life insurance sales person can present the potential policyholder's situation in such a way that they will want to buy the means by which their circumstances can be improved.

It is fun and exciting to take a concept and place it in front of a family who are at risk, or who want to accumulate wealth for some future event and have them understand the principles of complex solutions in an easy manner.

YOUR PERSONAL MOUNTAIN

Simplicity makes the point.

It is said that the best comedians have the art of "one liners".

The shaggy dog story which goes on for ever and has a dubious punch line can very often fall flat, but the one liner

"I shot an elephant in my pyjamas yesterday"

"How did you get the elephant in your pyjamas in the first place?" hits the spot.

Those who seek, or require life assurance, permanent health insurance, or retirement schemes, do not want to know the minute detail of such schemes at the initial stages. They want to see the concept, the heart, the kernel, to fondle the benefit in their mind, to feel the cosy glow of security, to experience the wonder of what it is all about.

This book is about one page presentations that lead to the solving of specific situations. To the creation of specific circumstances; put fire in the belly of the deliverer of the message and the recipient and thus motivate both to action.

We all have mountains to climb, our own personal mountains, but what does yours look like?

Do you climb your mountain to the accompaniment of water tinkling down a meadow backed hillside, lush green with the sounds of animals and birds in the background, the warm glow of the sun on the flowers. Do the flowers wave at you as you pass? Is your mountain pleasurable, comfortable, warm and unhurried....?

Or is your mountain more like the north face of the Eiger, cold, grey, stark, with nothing but the sound of a biting wind moaning across the crevices and driving against you as you struggle to keep your foothold, and hammer another spike into the cold stark exterior in an attempt to lift you further up its vertical face? Does it have to be exhilarating because of its difficulty? Its sheer awkwardness and challenge? Is this your mountain?

When we start on our professional way, we each have our own mountain which we all hear, see and feel in a different way, that is unique to us. However, we do have to assess the mountain, no matter how big or small it may be, for making mountains out of molehills, creating superlative results from common or garden ordinary resources takes skill, effort, strategy, planning and execution.

In the coronation year of Queen Elizabeth II, Edmund Hillary [later Sir Edmund] mounted an expedition to reach the summit of Mount Everest. Hillary did not see Mount Everest as his first challenge but I am sure he saw it as his ultimate goal. He probably started by climbing hills in the Dales or Downs of New Zealand, practising his skills, honeing his technique.

In that final assault he used Sherpas, expert mountain guides, who knew the winds, the snow, the drifts, the movements, the ideal places to make camp, to store supplies and reserves and thus ensure his success.

How many times has it been said that professional people never plan to fail - they just fail to plan. Speakers on a thousand platforms throughout the world have made that observation and listeners have failed to heed to the veracity of the message.

This publication endeavours to transfer my passion for my profession as a life assurance salesman to you by means of one-pagers that, hopefully, will do for you what the R.A.C. and A.A. route maps do for motorists wishing to get from Arbroath to Aberystwyth, from Manchester to Milton Keynes, or from Lincoln to Land's End.

The technicalities of the route are pushed to one side. It is displayed in the most simplistic and conceptual manner so as to assist the individual in grasping the fundamentals of the route to be taken and the benefits to be drawn from it. What must be expended to achieve the destination is also clarified and rendered down to its most understandable form.

People only want to know WHAT IT COSTS and WHAT ARE THE BENEFITS.

DO NOT CONFUSE ME WITH THE FACTS, IT IS WHAT I PERCEIVE THAT IS THE TRUTH.

Thus, when we set out to reach the summit of our mountain, we should seek a summit that is pleasurable to us, and a route that is within our grasp though interesting enough to be stimulating and to stretch our capabilities.

My endeavour here is to make your mountain easier to climb and more enjoyable during the journey.

Whilst I am sure that some of the ideas are not new to you, it is hoped that they will give new vision to your future plans. Put passion into your voice. Lend enthusiasm to your endeavours.

As life assurance professionals you hold in trust the responsibility for storing the financial lifeblood of the clients that you serve, in readiness for disaster, if and when it strikes. When their mountains crumble, their route to their summit becomes blocked and they fall from that precipitous climb, you will have provided the safety rope.

Like the National Blood Transfusion Service or Sir Edmund Hillary's base camps, that store of life giving financial blood, of essential life saving material, will be there in place ready to use as and when it is needed.

The following chapters are a contribution to your success. I wish you well with your mountain and wish you success in your journey to your own summit and the ever taller peaks that are to follow it throughout your career.

Making Mountains out of Molehills

I started with minus £1,000. A £1,000 overdraft which brought me a black, leather interior Austin Cambridge for £450, a decent leather attaché case and a house full of second-hand furniture. I well remember that three piece suite. The second tier of cushions missing, you needed a crane to get out of it as one was effectively sat on the floor.

That was twenty years ago. L.I.S. Limited, a national insurance brokerage that dealt primarily with Forces personnel [and later expanded to become part of the Pioneer Mutual Group], trained me in the basic rudiments of life insurance and I owe them a great debt of gratitude for their enthusiastic support, especially Dave Fern who was the Regional Manager. Bill Scriven who literally picked me up off the door-step and said "How would you like to sell life assurance, son?", and of course, Terry Clark, the managing director of L.I.S. and a man of great vision.

There are others in my life before this time that I would like to thank and I dedicate this book to:

Noreen Louis
Ann Middleditch's dad.
Harry Hawks
Mr Dawes
Corny Cornealias
Mr Dyson.

The last four gave me tremendous support during my secondary education and brought me to heights that my one parent family [took me off the potty too early] existence should have denied me.

Another great influence on my life was Warrant Officer Varty who oversaw most of my technical training as an engineer at Royal Air Force Halton. Yes, in amongst all the other things, I am an ex BRAT.

What has all this got to do with molehills? Moles live underground and that is where I started. Beneath the surface. £1,000 in debt plus a mortgage [which oddly enough I do not consider as a debt - it's a bit like terminal rent to me] and yet I had a mountain to climb. One mountain - you're joking. Dozens and dozens of mountains to climb. Some of them more than once. But fortunately on only one occasion with a near fatal injury. Pride comes before a fall, and I had my fall in October, 1987.

I think that I have experienced life in the broadest possible sense, my job is to deliver "good" to replace "bad". Blessings not curses.

Every life insurance salesman's job is to deliver "good". The funeral director, the solicitor who sorts out the Estate, the banker who may well wind everything up and the accountant who draws a line at the bottom of the page, **all take their fee.**

That is when the life insurance salesman delivers "good"; brings the blessings to override the course of a "disaster"

The life assurance professional is a bit like the wonderful corps of nurses who work for the National Blood Transfusion Service. Just as blood is the essential ingredient for keeping a physical body alive, so money is the blood of financial life, both domestic and business.

The life assurance professional stores the excess life blood just in case a transfusion is needed at some later date. The only difference between the National Blood Transfusion Service and life insurance companies is that you do not have to be a 'donor' to receive a blood transfusion when you need it.

Many a time during my career I have had the feeling that I was being looked upon as Dracula's double. Certainly the way the Financial Services Act is written and implemented, one could be forgiven for feeling that way.

The self gratification of the vampire has little in common with the Blood Transfusion Service. Self gratification has little to do with the life assurance professional either.

I am proud to be a life assurance salesmen. Through the efforts of myself and my colleagues, I have seen many families kept together and many businesses saved from failure, just by the mere presence of what Ben Feldman would call a 'piece of paper', 'a drop of ink' and a 'promise to pay'.

That is what this book is all about and I hope and trust that you will not only enjoy it, but you will find inspiration, passion, motivation and a challenge for life through the course of its pages.

Mountains out of Molehills

CONTENTS

Fireside Mole

=1=

A FINANCIAL
TRANSFUSION

"What's this?" I ask

I draw a stick man lying down on a stick bed and then I ask
the question again.

"What's this?"

"Well it's someone in a bed", is the reply, if I am lucky.

"That's right, and what is this?"

Then I draw a "gallows" over the head end of the bed and I
draw a bottle on the end of the downward stroke of the gallows,
hanging over the person and half fill it with "liquid" and draw a
line down into the person's arm.

"Ah! they are in hospital"

"That's right" "Someone in hospital getting a blood
transfusion"

"But where does the blood come from?"

A quizzical look

"No seriously, where does the blood come from?"

"Well donors"

"Yes that's correct"

On the righthand side of this A4 sheet of paper - [I have started
on the lefthand side], I draw a stick man and a stick women and
I write underneath "donors"

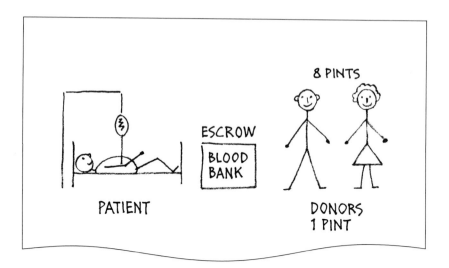

Then I might say, "Well that is O.K. we have donors here and the patient here, but what fits in between?"

Again a quizzical look.

"Well do we hang the donor up and take a pipe from their arm and put it into the patient's arm as if were syphoning petrol or something like that?"

"Oh no, it comes from a blood bank"

"Aha - a bank, that is really the key word, isn't it, bank"

"Now, in fact, all banks do is hold money in escrow. If we look up the word escrow it means to hold on deposit or put in safe keeping, for when it is required. So the blood donors provide blood; they have eight pints of blood normally. One pint is taken out, an armful in Tony Hancock terms, deposited in the blood bank, so when somebody needs it, the blood is there ready to use".

"But blood comes in different types doesn't it?" "We have rhesus positive and RH negative and all of these other things. A and O and stuff, so we need to keep all of these different types of blood available all of the time, in the blood bank for when it is needed" Mine is OH Positive.

Now we have said that banks keep money in escrow. That is also what insurance companies do, so if we turn this scenario around; we change "eight pints" to "£80" and the "one pint" to "£10". Let's put that £10 in escrow, a financial blood bank, which is the insurance company, so that when disaster strikes, we have the financial life blood to inject into the family unit if **dad dies or mum dies.**

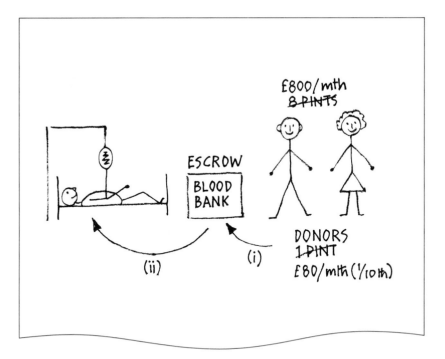

We have now discribed the basic principle of life assurance protection.

The analogy with a blood transfusion service and life assurance does not end there.

The urgency of the situation is also paramount. Whether we are sales people or technicians, administrators or clerks in life insurance just as in blood bank situations, we have to make sure that the financial life blood is available when disaster strikes.

Every member of the community is not a blood donor, however we all expect to be able to draw on resources that will keep us alive if a major road accident occurs or we are having surgery.

To be part of the financial blood transfusion service we have to contribute to the fund, each and every one of us, and we can only draw off from the fund in proportion to our contribution. The primary point here is that we have to "contribute" even if it is only the "first ten pounds".

We do not have to contribute a "pint" to get a "pint" of life giving financial blood.

Urgency is important. Can you imagine somebody who needs radical emergency surgery being rushed into hospital and only at that point does somebody say -

"Well - what sort of blood group is he or she?" OH positive and with that:

"Well let's go and find somebody, I think Nellie at number 93 down the road is that blood group, let's go down and get a pint of hers and I think Fred at number 47 is also that, just nip down and get his"

Can you imagine staff wandering around as if it will do tomorrow, whilst in the meantime the patient is dying?

In the financial sense a family or a business can easily die, or become seriously disabled, if treatment is not administered promptly and in the right quantity. The urgency of having an appropriate amount of the right "blood group", financial blood in escrow at the appropriate time, is essential.

Nobody has a lease on life. You, the reader, could be in a local hospital in five minutes time. You could be in the morgue in five minutes time. They are the facts of life.

As life assurance professionals it is our task and our duty to ensure that people do not procrastinate about putting a little of their "excess" income away today to ensure that there is a financial sufficiency if those who would take out our policy die too soon, live too long or become disabled.

We all have to generate the motivating force to make people act promptly. I get regular correspondence from the National Blood Transfusion Service asking me to donate blood. To my shame, I never seem to get down to the hospital or the hall where the blood doning service operates from, even though it is only twenty minutes from my office. I can see the need and I know that it would do good. I also know that I would not miss the pint of blood because my body will soon make it up. We don't miss the "pint" of financial blood either. Our system soon makes it up.

However, if there was an accident and I was drawn into that set of circumstances, and could see the need so clearly that I was motivated beyond my present state, then I would most certainly make the donation. Now it may be that they bring the blood transfusion service to within two minutes walk of my office, which is where they used to have it, so that I do not need to exert myself too much, then I would give more readily.

That is the way we all are about most things, that is why life assurance has to be sold to most people. It is sought by very few.

As life assurance professionals we have to explain the financial blood donating service and we have to take the means to make the donation to the individuals concerned and assist them in every way possible to ensure that on the day they need that financial life blood, there is some in escrow in a life insurance company for their family, dependents, business colleagues or whoever - and it may be themselves - to draw upon.

Widow Mole

2

INDIVIDUAL FINANCIAL PLANNING

In the book "You Sign" , the principles of life assurance are discussed in some detail, using drawings.

I passionately believe that if you cannot put a presentation on one sheet of paper and make it intelligible, then forget the presentation. It is too complicated, it is too hard for the majority of people to understand. People "buy" concepts NOT PRODUCTS, Concepts, beliefs, feelings, images - that is what people buy.

I do not deny that there are many people who demand figures, who demand graphs, who demand to know what it is all about. In my experience, those people only get to the point where they want those figures, graphs and explanations once they have seen and identified the basic need. The basic concept is what it does NOT how it works.

To many people, life assurance is a very poor investment.

Of course, life assurance was never designed as an investment vehicle. It is a means of protection. Protection is boring, but let me ask you a question. You are on a world cruise on the "Canberra" or the "Sea Princess" and at the beginning of the voyage you notice that there are no lifeboats.

When the Purser should be saying;

"We are now going to give you some instruction in how to use your life jackets", the Purser says, instead

"I just want to tell you all that due to economies we are cutting back and are only providing the essentials for the voyage,like food and drink.

We have dispensed with life jackets and have not bothered to repair the lifeboats. But have removed them to save weight and accommodate more passengers."

Would I be right in assuming that you would feel a little uncomfortable at that point?

Perhaps you holiday in Tenerife or an even more exotic location abroad.You get involved with "Air Traffic Control" getting all those aeroplanes into all those "air corridors"; all going in the same direction at different heights and boring things like that.

I mean, SURELY, if we did away with "Controllers" that would bring the air fares down. While we are about it, let's get rid of those red fire engines at the airport - I mean, hell, they are never used are they? Nobody ever crashes; they are just an unnecessary extravagance!"

Sounds familiar? Is there a similarity in not having lifeboats, life jackets or fire engines, and life assurance?

Insurance keeps people in neat lines, it shoulders the financial responsibility when a disaster occurs. The financial lifeblood that a life assurance contract provides has to be put into the client's perspective.

Lifeboats are of absolutely no use whatsoever.....until. It is also worth noting that they are always provided to over capacity. The perspective that determines their requirement is the fear of people drowning, not of sailing in a boat.

By outlining an individual's financial life in a way that he or she can identify and by clearly showing on a one-page presentation what usually happens to a nineteen year old throughout his or her life in financial terms, you will undoubtedly unlock the door to that individuals perspective concerning why and how personal protection plus savings should be carried out.

Once I have finished my initial fact-find with any individual, the first question I ask is:

"How much can you comfortably afford to save out of your

regular income, including building society, bank and what have you"?

I then keep quiet.

You see most people have not been asked that question before. They need time for it to register and think it through; think about it and make some sort of intelligible response.

"er... £50 per month or £15 per week."

Now you can start helping them further.

"Does that include the car breaking down? Shouldn't you have a contingency for that?"

"I put that to one side separately"

"Well, fine, add that in, let's make sure we have a proper view of everything that you are doing. "Does that include holidays?" I ask.

"Well no, I have put that away in the Building Society already so I didn't really include that"

"Everything has to be accounted for in our figures before we can look at planning your financial life"

I then make a very important statement:

SAVE £150 PER mth
MAX. ⅓ LIFE ASS.
£50/mth

"I do not believe that any individual should put any more than one-third of his or her saveable income into life assurance products, with the exception perhaps of a domestic mortgage."

"Bearing in mind we can put two-thirds of your saveable income away for short term projects and the safety fund. Do you think that this is sensible?"

Sensible - the person that you are talking to probably thought that you were going to put everything you could lay your hands on into a commission paying product that would do him no good at all! You are actually demonstrating that you are looking after his best interests. All manner of short term savings can be discussed and described or he can be left to his own resources. They have been mentioned and they are of prime importance.

With the other one-third of saveable income we can now look at the person's long term goals, and I ask the simple question "What age will you be next birthday?"

Wait for the answer

"Er - twenty"

"Here is your life line" and I draw it on a sheet of paper "I am going to assume that you survive to your next birthday.

"What other event on this life line, YOUR life line, can you

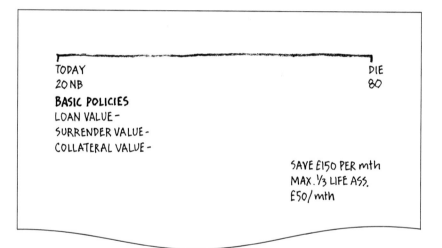

say is definitely going to happen?" Then be quiet. Let the person think. After a minute of good solid silence, I say

"The only event that will **definitely** happen on your life line I would suggest; is death"

I mark the right hand end of the line "die": D I E.

I then say to the individual,

"I do not believe in financial planning just for the sake of it. We should always endeavour to plan for specific events, which means that we can actually plan for the financial result of your dying, whenever that occurs."

"You will be pleased to know that the average male lives to age eighty".

The look of relief on the person's face, on occasions, has to be seen to be believed. But they are off the hook. They have a while to go yet!

However, the picture is still in front of them "How do we cater for death?" A question that I answer myself, "we use a whole life policy. There is no other vehicle anywhere that has ever been invented by man that can provide cash at **any** time that death occurs, other than a whole life policy. It guarantees payment. Remember, we do not know when a person will die, but we do know that they will."

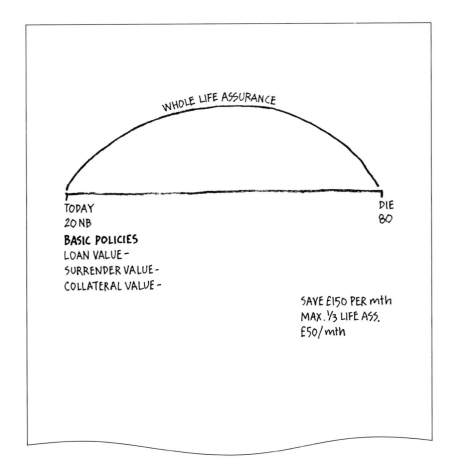

I then draw an "umbrella" line from one end of the "life line" to the other.

I turn back to the individual and now ask:

"If we know that you are going to live to age eighty, on average, what other point on your life line can we definitely plan for? What is another major milestone in your life when **you** will need cash?"

This question usually invokes a fairly prompt answer. "Retirement",
And I say, "that's great", and draw a second "umbrella" line within the first.

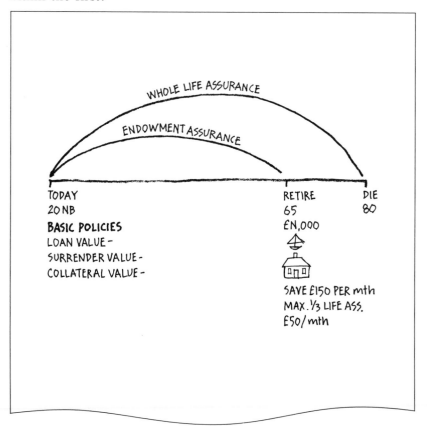

Now the difference between death and retirement is that at death someone else wants the money whilst at retirement it is all for you. I draw a little picture of a boat and a cottage in the country and say,

"There you go, when you retire you will probably want to get a boat, buy a cottage in the country, just put your feet up and relax, is that right?"

I stop and wait for an answer.

"So we want lots of money for you, the individual, at that time"

I draw two "umbrellas". One which represents the whole life policy, which goes from '**TODAY**' (twenty next birthday), through to age eighty and '**DIE**'. I do another umbrella which runs from today to age sixty-five.

Take a Break

My next comment is to address the major item of house purchase, which can occur at any time between now and retirement. If home ownership is a positive aspiration of this particular person then, of course, that can be taken into account now in providing future benefit. For people who are already married or have a family, then perhaps school fees planning, house purchase, parent care, vintage car or luxury yacht purchase may all come into consideration. The important thing, in my view, is that they form part of a structured analysis.

Term assurance is also discussed as a means of covering short term borrowing, or specific short term liabilities such as children. The idea is to create a montage of insurances that provide for specific, planned or foreseeable events in the most economic fashion.

A further "umbrella" is inserted within the first two to represent the Term Insurance policy plan.

With my umbrella graph now complete at the top of the page, and taking up approximately the top half, I set about the bottom half of my single page A4 presentation.

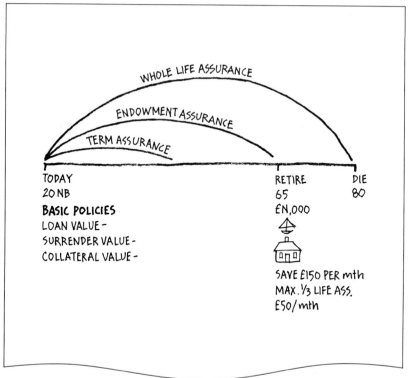

I continue:

"Let us look at the life line again."

I draw a "life line" in the bottom one-third of the page and follow through synchronising my illustration with my words; thus building up a life's liabilities graph.

Here you are age twenty and here you are dead at eighty" [I hope that I am not going to be accused of subliminal programming through the pages of this book and the people who use this presentation]. "What events are likely to happen on your life line?"

"I can only judge by what has happened to other people in my experience, and in my experience a twenty year old man is quite happy putting away large slices of his income. If he has no money he just stays at home. There comes a day when "she" walks into his life and that is when liabilities soar and saveable income can become somewhat diminished. With the advent of a spouse, there usually comes a mortgage or at least rented accommodation and the possibility, of course, of children. That is why we build a buffer and only use one-third of your saveable income now in other than short term investments."

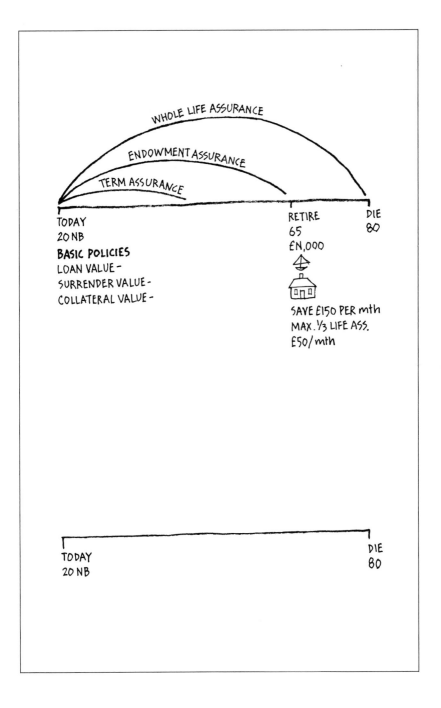

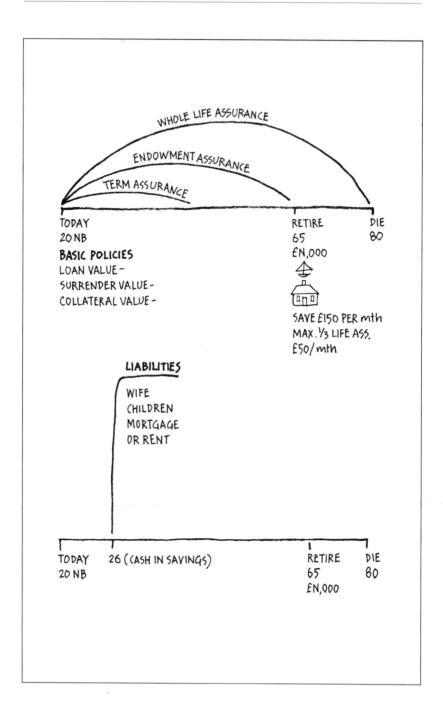

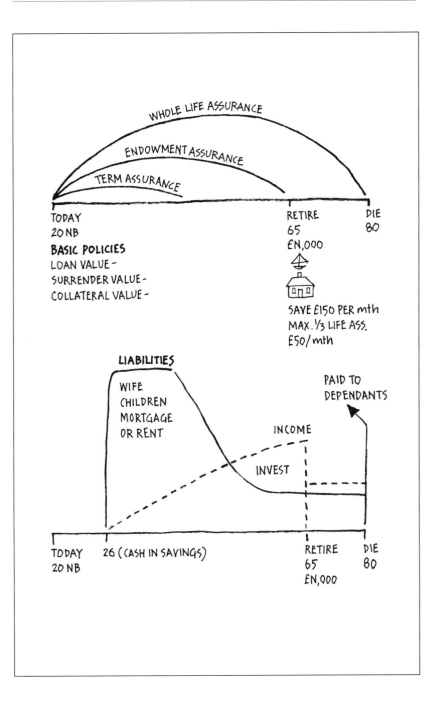

I have a persistency rate of over 90%, as I have stated, that is because lapses are sold at the proposal stage of a policy. By concentrating on specific financial targets which the individual can identify with, the "LIFE LINE" becomes part of the solution.

The subsequent plans that clients make all follow the same line. You must adopt and adapt to your own style and perception.

Ask yourself - what works for me?

I then go on to explain that as liabilities reduce the children get older, more income is generated within the household as both spouses are working, and probably getting promoted, then we can change our protective environment into an investment environment, and look to retirement.

I suggest that we have at least a proportion of the available savings going into an investment contract, either to buy a house or to look to retirement.

The person can see some money coming back - a return for their efforts.

Look to a proportion of the cover being on a whole life basis to make sure that cash is available at age eighty to pay for a reasonable funeral. That is what life assurance is all about. Not term assurance that runs out before you do. Remember only 2% of all term insurance ever pays a claim value and 95% of all investments are never around for the future because we had access to them and SPENT THEM TODAY!

So there we have it, a basic insurance philosophy that incorporates saving and financial planning in all its facets for a life time. In the following chapters we will look at more specific one-pager presentations and again look at perspective and where the client perceives the benefit is coming from.

Seaside Mole

═ 3 ═

JUST LITTLE BOXES OF MONEY

Over my professional career I have examined many methods of providing widows and widowers with sufficient financial resources to replace what has been lost through the death of a father or provide what is required, in financial terms, to partially substitute the wide ranging and essential role of a mother.

The forces required, financially, in earning a living and raising children are diametrically opposed. To conduct one's work effectively requires concentration, single-mindedness, enthusiasm, time and dedication.

The same attributes are required, but pulling in the opposite direction, to successfully bring up children. My father was a master tailor. Dad had to spend most of his time working to earn enough money to bring me up after I lost my mother at the age of four. There was no insurance. Dad did not believe in it!

Family Income Benefit is instalment term assurance. BOXES OF MONEY SET ASIDE FOR EACH YEAR AND EACH CHILD UNTIL THEY ATTAIN, SAY, AGED TWENTY.

The concept is simple. Here is your lifeline and here is a temporary liability that will one day grow up and leave home, it is called a child!

"What do you want to achieve for your children?"

Let your clients tell you what they want to achieve

"And how will you achieve that?"

Then let the clients tell you how they are going to achieve whatever it is.

"What if one of you died between now and when John goes to university? Who would look after the children?"

"I know that Mary is qualified but why should your children lose both their father and their mother at the same time. Their father because he has just died, and their mother because she HAS to go out to work"

"May I show you a simple and inexpensive means of creating income and the financial freedom to make the choice which was so important in Jane's case. She did not HAVE to do anything when she became a widow. Jane had freedom of CHOICE. Isn't that what you would want Mary to have?

"The concept is quite simple. Here is your lifeline, all we do is create boxes on money for every year until Adrian and Gemma both reach age twenty.

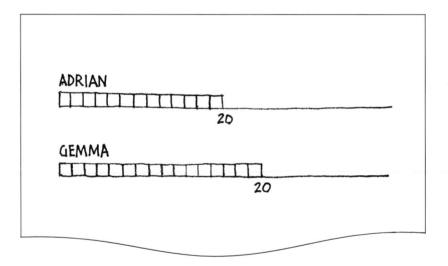

You draw two lines on a blank A4 sheet of paper. You fill out the required number of boxes, being careful to count them out for the appropriate number for each child's twentieth year.

"Now, for each year that you survive we delete a box [put a cross in each box as you talk, three to five will be sufficient] and I sincerely hope that all of them are reduced to rubble, because that means you have survived, which I personally think is important."

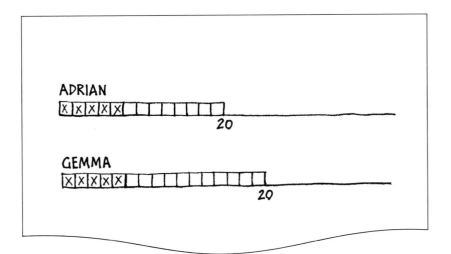

"However, if you die,"

And, about year five, you would draw a line down from the lifeline, through the two lines, and write the word "die" at the bottom of it.

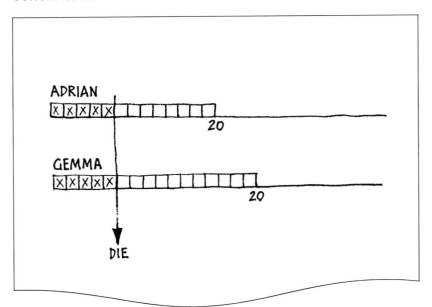

"Then the insurance company would pay out the boxes for the remainder of the period to Adrian and Gemma's twentieth birthday".

"Now the nice thing about this scheme is that whilst the premium remains level, we increase the value of the box by 5% compound for every year from inception, thus at least to some degree, keeping pace with inflation.''

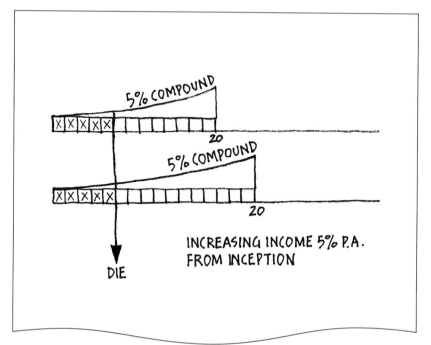

The policy is placed in a flexible trust, a box if you like, which means that all that is required on death, is a Death Certificate and the policy. The income can be paid straight to the surviving spouse.

"The other benefit of this type of arrangement is that if both of you die at the same time, as might happen in a road accident, then both policies will pay out to the guardians of the children [assuming of course that you have both got current Wills and we know who the guardians are] to enable them to bring up your children up without worrying about the financial resources to do so."

"Does that sound like something you would like to do?" Very often there is a question which is asked of by either one, or both parties

"Is there any cash back at the end?"

The answer, of course, is "No"

If you judge this is important to the couple concerned, then you can proceed as follows

"No, this is a pure insurance to cover the specific risk at the lowest possible cost."

"How much would you want to add to that contribution to ensure that all your premiums are returned - **may we double it?**"

For my part, I have to admit, that I try to talk people out of getting cash back at the end of the contract because I see it as a stand alone and very individual requirement for them to take on. If the WANT is for a cash sum at the end - give it to them. Bolt on an endowment. Always give what THEY want not what **you** think that they should have.

It may be that you are only able to deal with a company, or companies, that do not underwrite Family Income Benefit type contracts. It may well be, however, that by using either segmented policies or an instalment based whole life contract you could derive something very similar to the increasing Family Income Benefit policy that I have described, and build in through the surrender value a return of the premiums at the end of the contract period.

The most important thing is to satisfy the perceived requirements of the individual that you are talking to.

The premiums should be quoted weekly as should the benefits. Many people think weekly [even though they do not think they do.] Explain the trust in simple terms also.

WHAT IS A TRUST?

"A Trust is just a box with a lid on it. The lid has got a slot in it through which we can pass things into the Trust through but we cannot take them out. The thing is that the contents of the box belong to specific people known as the beneficiaries and the box is looked after by people called Trustees.

The Trustees have the key to the box but they would only normally open the box on the happening of a specific event. They are there primarily to see that nobody tampers with the contents of the the box.

What we are putting inside the box is the proceeds of a life insurance policy. If it is a family income benefit policy then it will be the monthly or quarterly income that comes out of the policy. If it is a whole life assurance or an endowment policy then it will be the lump sum that goes into the Trusts for distribution comes

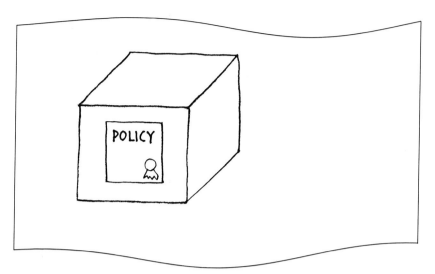

out. The Trustees are responsible for that.

Each month contributions are put into the box, the Trustees look after it and then at the end of the day, specific people benefit from the Trust called the beneficiaries. That is all a Trust is.

The nice thing is that the Trust keeps the proceeds secure for someone else, maybe your spouse, your children, business partner, whoever.

We can have a "Flexible Trust" which allows us to change the beneficiaries with the consent of all the Trustees and you, Mr Client, will be one of the Trustees. We can change the beneficiaries to suit changing circumstances".

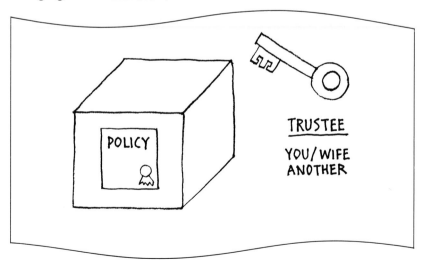

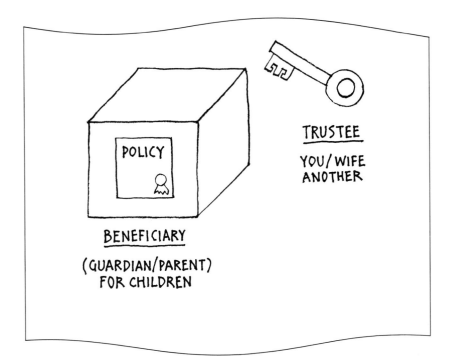

The death of one spouse will require us to change the beneficiary[ies] under the surviving spouse's policy to the children and we can do that without any difficulty.

Policies that are written in a Trust do not need to be dealt with through Probate or Letters of Administration. All that is normally required by the insurance company is the policy document and the death certificate.

Where pure protection policies are involved, such as family income benefit or term insurance, the policy is of no value to the life assured in any event, therefore, placing them in trust is a most sensible course of action - a flexible trust of course.

Case Study 1

I well remember when Peter and Janet came to see me to arrange their mortgage.

It was many years ago now, but I still remember it quite vividly. They came into my office and we discussed their preparations for buying the house, looked to a solicitor, and compared the repayment principle and interest and endowment methods of repaying a mortgage. They settled for the Low Cost Endowment Interest Only route. Everything was signed up and sorted out.

Peter and Janet had two daughters aged eight and ten, and it was November time.

"Now what are we going to do about these two little girls" I said.

"For £2.50 a week we can provide little boxes of money so that if anything happens to Janet, you Peter, will be able to employ a housekeeper so that you can carry on with your lorry driving. You know you have to be out early most mornings, and there are some nights when you get home very late". "You will need to know that the girls are being properly looked after"

If anything happens to Peter, you Janet, will need some income." "It is always a tragedy when children lose not only their father through death, but also their mother because she is forced to go out to work to support them. The loss of two parents is unnecessary with a Family Income Benefit policy."

There are occasions when we don't like to push too hard. Peter and Janet were quite firm in their resolve not to take out the life insurance at that time.

"Let us just wait until we get settled into the new house and can see what our expenses are, then we will talk about this insurance, say next year. Let's wait six months"

"Alright" I said, "I will make an appointment now in my book for May," and in my planner diary for the 12th May the following year I wrote Peter and Janet, Family Income Benefit".

None of us have a lease on life. In January of the following year, I received a 'phone call from a mutual friend - "can Janet come in and see you, Peter has died?"

Peter, a thirty-nine year old lorry driver, had had a heart attack and died a few days later.

Janet came to see me. I remember that quite vividly too. She shed her grief on my office carpet.

"I came to see you", she said, **"you are the only person I could think of who could help"**

We were able to help. I stated that we had arranged a Low Cost Endowment policy and the death benefit would pay off the mortgage.

Janet and her two daughters had a house to live in. However, Janet still had to go out to work as a secretary to earn the bread and butter for the table.

I often reflect, if only I had pushed a little harder to get that Family Income Benefit policy in place for each of them, at a cost of just £2.50 per week, how much better it would have been for the family unit. How much easier it would have been for Janet to cope: and all for as little as £2.50 per week!!

Case Study 2

By contrast I should perhaps tell you about Jane and Brian.

I was an engineer in the Royal Air Force and Brian was one of my lads. He came through my hands during his training and later in his career was a Sergeant Engineer.

In between times, I had left the Royal Air Force, having taken up my studies to join the life assurance profession and he became one of my prospects for life insurance in those early days. The early seventies.

Brian was a keen ralliest with a super wife, Jane and I well remember, following the birth of their daughter, that I sought to top up Brian's Whole Life Policy with Family Income Benefit. Little boxes of Term Assurance. Also to put some in place for Jane.

Brian, as a ralliest, compared the cost of the life assurance to the cost of bits for his rally car.

The interviews were never that easy because, of course, the contributions to the insurance fund had to be justified. On this occasion common sense prevailed by means of my simple drawings, and they understood as a couple, that the boxes of money were there for their daughter Alison [indirectly through the surviving parent].

None of us ever think that these policies are going to pay out.

It was several years later when I got the telephone call to say that Brian had been working on an armoured plated vehicle on a raised platform, only about six feet above the ground, when he had toppled backwards and cracked his skull on the concrete floor.

He was in a coma for eight days and mercifully died.

When you are in tied accommodation, it is very easy to think that it is yours and no matter how much sympathy is felt by an employer, it still did not stop the letter coming to say:

" We regret to hear of the death of your husband. You have sixty days in which to vacate your Married Quarter".

Brian's parents said to Jane that she could go and stay with them. Her own parents also offered her accommodation.

"Come and stay with us", they said.

Jane is not fiercely independent, but the life assurance that we had set up for her, those little boxes of money, and the capital sum from that Whole Life Policy provided her with a home of her own, and income that would last through to Alison's twentieth birthday. To some extent the income was inflation proofed by a 5% escalation provision.

Jane did not HAVE to go and stay with anybody. **Life assurance gave her the choice and independence that every widow or widower deserves.**

Jane has not worked since her husband's death. She has always been at home to be a mother to her daughter, and that is the way she wants it. The price of that security was a mere couple of pounds per week.

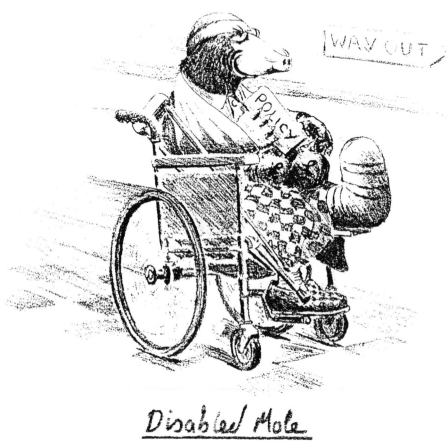

Disabled Mole

4

WHAT WILL YOU DO WHEN YOU ARE OFF SICK?

Have you ever thought about being disabled? Not able to work? Not able to do what you do today and earn the money that you earn today?

You have probably thought about it but dismissed the idea as preposterous. It is something that happens to other people. They are the sort of people who take part in the international Special Olympics or are sponsored by MENCAP or....., but it is never "me". Could it **ever** be you?

Statistically, I have to tell you that there is a very high possibility that it will be "you". Because if you are between the ages of thirty and sixty-five then 50% of your category of person is likely to be disabled for a two year period. Between now and your age sixty-five - statistically!

The prospect is even less pleasant when you think about the financial consequences of that statement.

Think about how you would explain that principle to somebody and then ask them to put away sufficient money to account for their liabilities.

Over the years I have tried all sorts of ways and have been fairly successful in putting into force numerous group and individual

Permanent Health Insurance schemes, but nevertheless I have still found that it is difficult to get the perception right in people's minds.

DON'T CONFUSE ME WITH FACTS, IT IS WHAT I PER-CEIVE THAT IS TRUTH.

That is a phrase that I coined many years ago and it stands the test of time. It is a person's perception that is important. How can we use a one page A4 sheet of paper to increase someone's awareness of the need for Permanent Health Insurance or disability cover and create its proper perspective in their mind? I resort to the job hunting dilemma or debate.

I am talking to a well paid young man in a restaurant where we were thrown together to share a meal because of lack of space. After a hesitant start to the conversation, it transpired that he is a senior executive on quite a substantial salary but his employer adopts the strategy "we will pay you what we think you are worth and you look after your own employee benefits".

"May I ask you a question?"

er, yes

"What happens to your income if you are off sick?"

"I don't know - I think I get paid for three months and then I guess I'm on my own"

"Would you mind if I showed you something?"

"Not at all"

"It is what I call my job [a] job [b] illustration. Being disabled is a very serious matter and not having any income when you are disabled is even more serious, wouldn't you agree"?

"Well, probably"

"If you were searching for a job at the moment and job [a] paid you £30,000 per annum, much like the one you are in now, and if you were unable to carry on your job through sickness or an accident, then you would be paid Statutory Sick Pay and your employer would make that up to full salary for three months, is that correct"?

"That is right"

"That is job [a]."

Job [a] pays £30,000 per annum with no payment by the employer in the event of a prolonged disability. Statutory Sick Pay is all that will be paid.

JOB A

£30,000

DISABILITY

$\underline{SSP}$ 28 wks

INVALID
BENEFIT

JOB B

£29,000

DISABILITY

£20,000

To AGE 65

I complete all of the details down the left hand side of the A4 sheet of paper as shown on the illustration. The illustration shows the contrast between employment pay and disability earnings.

I now write on the right hand side of the A4 sheet, job [b],

"Now job [b] pays only £29,000 per annum. However, you would get £20,000 per annum until you are aged sixty-five if you were subject to a permanent disability, broken spine, heart attack, that sort of thing."

"Which job would you take?"

I then keep quiet.

The odd thing is that I have never had anybody choose job [a]. Not one.

That is the principle of Permanent Health Insurance. The client has agreed the level of contribution and the period of cover for the contract.

Do a full fact find, establish the earnings, establish the terms of the "contract of employment" and how the employee would be paid in the event of disability [the same applies to partners in a partnership and their Partnership Agreement]. Know your Permanent Health Insurance rate book so that you can apply an appropriate premium in round figures. KNOW THE STATU-TARY SICK PAYMENTS - S.S.P. IS PAID FOR TWENTY-EIGHT WEEKS - benefits vary year on year.

Always quote a little higher than you need to be so that when you do the actual figures, they work out cheaper on the illustration.

Take a photocopy of you A4 sheet of paper illustration and make sure that the client has a copy for their records. They will never, ever question why they bought that insurance, they will know. They elected to take a job with a slightly lower salary but a much better fringe benefit.

THEY INVARIABLY CHOOSE SECURITY.

Derek is a very dear friend of mine. He was a solicitor, well I suppose he still is really, one cannot take that away from him.

Derek approached me many years ago to look into the provision of disability income for his partners in a major practice. We obtained details all of the partners, drew up the relevant schedules, together with a report, delivered them to the partnership secretary and then it all went quiet. Does it ever go quiet for you?

History has taught me that when things go quiet, there is usually trouble afoot. Sure enough the partnership broke up some eighteen months later. Derek, aged fifty-two, and a twenty-seven year old partner took three offices and set up, which was in effect, their own firm.

During the late summer I approached Derek to review his personal insurances and the first point that I made to him was his severe lack of disability insurance. If he was ill, for a protracted period, his family would be in dire straits. By the November of that year, I had put together some figures, went to see Derek but he was obviously under a fair amount of stress to get the business moving and establish himself in his new two man partnership.

"I want to leave everything until the New Year, Terry" he said.

"Let's make it March when I have got my first year's trading figures out and we can see exactly where we are going, and what money there is to spare"

"This is not about money to spare Derek, this is about the future of your family if you are disabled"

"Don't press me" he said. "I've got a lot on at the moment, I had a medical in May, I am fully fit, we will review everything in March, but please don't push me"

"Alright, Derek" said I, and I turned to leave, calling back as I went, "but don't get sick between now and next March"

January, oh January, why do you haunt me.

My friend Derek was sat eating his evening meal at a Rotary dinner when he slid slowly sideways off his chair. A stroke had taken his agility in a matter of seconds.

My fine upright friend, dropped into the abyss of despair. Derek blamed himself for not having provided that Permanent Health Insurance.

Was it his failing, or mine?

Derek had a young daughter just starting secondary school and a twenty-one year old at university. Major family rearrangements had to be made.

The family house was sold and they moved into a smaller one. The original large garden was too much for even the dedicated gang of personal family friends who had endeavoured to keep under control. Pauline had to go back out to full time teaching, and that new solicitors partnership had to be dissolved.

If Derek was my failure, then I have to hold Bill Ryder up as my Olympic Flame.

Bill was a partner in a twelve man Estate Agency partnership when he had his stroke. I well remember the stories of Bill sat in a shed at the bottom of the garden doing his studies for his examinations.

The day Bill was taken ill we had a Group Permanent Health arrangement in place for his partnership that provided benefits after fifty-two weeks. I will not go into all the gory details but Bill had a stroke, another and another. He was severely disabled and latterly hospitalised for a long number of years, during which time his loving wife Pat was able to visit him daily. She did not have to worry where the money was coming from to run the house, or who was going to pay to get her three youngsters through university.

Had Permanent Health Insurance not been in place, the moral and financial obligations to the partnership, would have been a heavy burden indeed. The insurance company took the strain.

Bill died, his ambitions for his children at least in part achieved, thanks to a simple A4 sheet presentation.

Getting Home

5

FOR WHOM THE BELL TOLLS

The medical profession have got a lot to answer for. At the beginning of the century the average male life span was forty-five years because of the huge toll taken by infant mortality and more importantly contagious diseases.

You probably would not remember, but the older generation would certainly know of someone who died from scarlet fever, whooping cough and probably tuberculosis. Tuberculosis was a scerge disease that killed thousands of people. It was highly contagious. I am sure you cannot remember, but others will confirm, that there were lots of sanatoriums set up specifically to deal with the effects of that devastating disease.

Polio, was another major killer and until very recently when the problem was addressed by Rotary International, the crop of children in Asia who fell victim to polio was enormous.

The need for life assurance at the turn of the century, and up until probably twenty years ago, was centred upon the very real fact that a bread winner within a family, which was usually the man of the house and the father of the children, was a tremendous financial asset whose loss to the family was devastating. Life assurance, or should we say death insurance, was vital to the family unit although burial policies were, for the most part, all that was available to the "masses". During the last twenty years, life assurance has moved on from being something that just paid out a nominal amount on death. Indeed, the life assurance industry has become known more for investment returns rather than for death benefits, even though nearly 5 million per day, everyday, every year is paid out to widows, widowers, orphans and businesses to help shore them up in a time of need.

However, the medical profession have changed the whole emphasis with regard to life assurance cover. You see, the average man used to die at aged forty-five, as I have said, but nowadays the average man from the general population will live until he is seventy-five. He will live well into retirement.

The emphasis on life assurance has moved away from the time when most people would be looking after their families to a time when the main consideration is the surviving spouse. "Help the Aged" have recently launched "Dignity in Death" as their way of addressing that particular problem. What the medical profession have done is to eliminate the vast majority of the contagious diseases and replaced them in human terms with degenerative diseases.

By degenerative diseases I mean heart and respiratory problems, cancer, kidney failure and so on.

There is a very subtle difference to the new situation in financial terms. When the old diseases were contracted, death resulted in a very short space of time. Today, two-thirds of those over the age of sixty-five are suffering from a life threatening medical condition and will live probably five or more years. Many people during their lives will, therefore, find that because they have fallen victim to a degenerative disease they will not work again and will not be able to achieve their life's ambitions, but they will be alive to experience that financial failure. That is the difference and we have the medical profession to thank for it.

Thankful we should be, of course, because life is a lot better and more certain these days than it ever was before. The life assurance industry set out to address the financial problem aused by the onset of 'critical illness' or, as some people call it, 'dread disease.' For a premium not far removed from ordinary life assurance premiums, an individual is now able to create a capital sum to go on a world cruise, to make sure that they see Jimmy or Sarah get through university. A lump sum that might pay off a loan which the spouse would otherwise inherit which will lift what otherwise would be a feeling of despair and despondency to satisfaction and comfort.

At the turn of the century, eighty per cent of all deaths were due to contagious disease. In 1992, eighty per cent of all deaths are caused by degenerative diseases and if you fall victim to one, you will probably survive a significant period of time, during which that "death" benefit paid in advance, will be a godsend.

Many people who find themselves in wheelchairs, such as stroke or accident victims have to spend quite large sums of money on modifying their accommodation, their car and if they took up wheelchair road racing, the special equipment required for that. Electric wheelchairs are not cheap but they are very functional for the severely handicapped. A simple accident can result in the need for tens of thousands of pounds to be expended just to live a "normal" life. I know a young man who was in a road traffic accident seven years ago and lost his sight. If you saw him in the street you would not give him a second glance or think he was disabled. He will probably never work again.

As ever increasing medical techniques; heart, lung and other organ transplants extend our lives, let us not get depressed about what might, or might not, happen to us. It is amazing how many people make reasonable recoveries and lead very active lives, given the financial resources to ensure that they have the right attitude for recovery.

Critical illness or dread disease insurance is just like a blood transfusion. It is money in the financial blood bank to be used when it is needed. We know that it is a proven thing to do. How much more important are you than those material things that you insure for accident or theft, most items of which you could probably live without. Try living without yourself?

For the cost of one good meal out for two per month you can live secure in the knowledge that the medical profession can extend your life without the effects bothering you adversely financially. If the solution is in place, the situation will never become a problem.

" What would you do if you were given six months to live, today?"

It is with those words that I introduce my presentation on critical illness to a potential client. The response varies, as does the time taken for that individual to contemplate the subject before making the response. Some indeed do not respond within a reasonable time scale and, therefore, I have to move into the second phase, of a presentation that I have devised.

On my A4 sheet of paper I write [whilst I am making the positive

statements]:
"In 1900, the average male lived forty-five years."
And I write down - MALE FORTY-FIVE YEARS.
"Eighty per cent of those males died of a disease"
and I write, continuing the line across the
page, DIED, DISEASE

1900 MALE 80% DIED DISEASE - QUICKLY
     45

---

and I say as I write "QUICKLY"
You see, Mr Jones, Tuberculosis, scarlet fever, polio any number
of diseases that were around then are almost unheard of today. In
those days, life insurance, as we probably still think about it, death
insurance, was the most necessary thing for the family because the
bread winner could disappear very quickly and leave a financial
vacuum.

Then I start writing again, and speaking at
the same time.

" In 1990 the average male age was seventy-five [well seventy-
four point six] but what is point four between friends? Medical
science has stretched a life span and enabled us to abuse our bodies
more and keep us alive longer when we start to [a] fall apart, heart
attack that sort of thing [write down FALL APART] or [b] run
amok, cancer, multiple sclerosis that type of thing"

1900 MALE 80% DIED DISEASE - QUICKLY
     45
1990 MALE 80% DIED WEARING OUT ‒ SLOWLY
     75   RUNNING AMOK

---

and then I and say "slowly"
"The problem today is that we linger and, therefore, the old

form of life insurance - death insurance, does not relate to current circumstances.''

"I posed you the question just now, what would you do if you were given six months to live, and the most common responses that I have had are:

"forget work and capitalise on whatever was due to me"   If the person is a director or partner in a firm, then you can go on

"That probably means taking your capital out of the firm which means your co-directors or partners will have to buy you out.''

I then draw on my A4 sheet of paper about half-way down a circle, I put the individual that I am talking to in the centre of it as a stick image and put my first tentacle out of the circle with little stick images depicting the number of partners in response to the question

"How many partners do you have?''

1900 MALE 80% DIED DISEASE - QUICKLY
45
1990 MALE 80% DIED WEARING OUT _ SLOWLY
75   RUNNING AMOK

BUY OUT

and then draw a line down with another little stick man and the words BUY OUT.

The second thing people have said by way of response is to make peace with their Maker, visit a guru, go to the Holy Lane, whatever, and I depict a shrine and write under it PEACE.

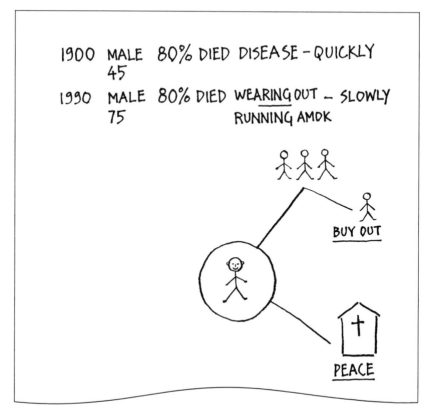

I then change the tempo a little bit and say the majority would probably say "well it is O.K. doing this accountancy, legal, architectural whatever work, but you wont catch me around making all the files up, bringing them all up to date - I'm off to have fun."

Whilst I have been talking I have actually drawn a cruise ship and written underneath it HAVE FUN.

The fourth tendril leads down to a sack. I look the prospect in the eye and I say

"A lot of people will become paraplegic or confined to a wheel chair, this is not a six months to live situation, this is more a set of circumstances where you have to widen the doors in the house, put in a chair lift, that type of thing. Get a special modification done to your car, or maybe just clear off the household debts or business overdraft"

Whilst talkingg a bag of money has been drawn and annotated 'PAY DEBT - ALTER HOUSE'.

At this point I usually tell the story of a colleague of mine who

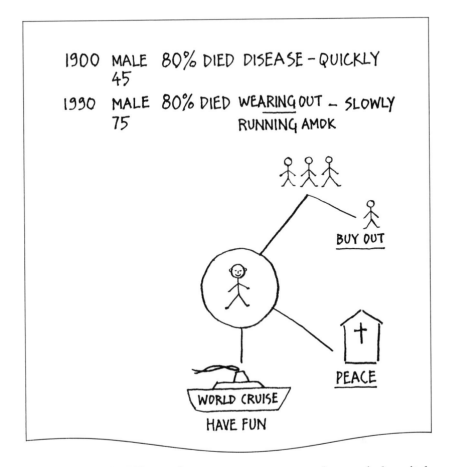

delivered a critical illness cheque to a young man who was in hospital dying. The young man was extremely concerned and pensive about what was going to happen to his indebtedness, even when my colleague arrived with a £30,000 cheque. However, at this point the young man got a pad and a pencil and allocated the £30,000 in various bits and pieces to pay off what he owed to people and the bank. My colleague said that once the paperwork had been done and the cheque had, in effect, been dispensed between all of the various creditors, the young man's physiology changed completely and he sank into a peace with himself, as if to say "I can go now - it is all sorted"

and then I remain quite for just a little while before going on to say

"You're married aren't you", and no appropriate response is forthcoming, "and you have children?" "yes four" he says.

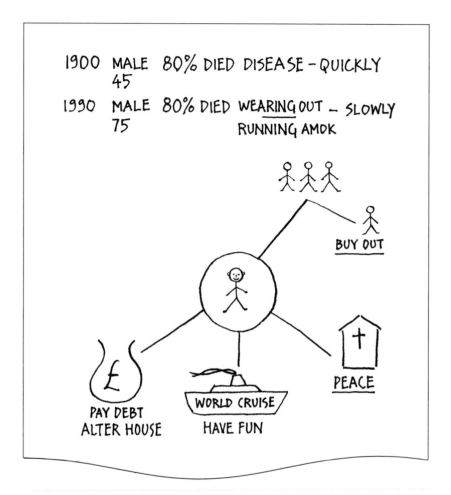

Whilst he or she is replying, I am drawing a little match stick wife and some little match stick children that are awfully like signs that relate to the answers.

It is all well and good being terminally ill and saying to your spouse

"don't worry, when I die there will be £200,000 for you to make sure you have plenty of income."

Anyone with any experience, particularly of widows, knows how vulnerable they are, how uncertain they are and how grief makes any decision making, particularly about money which has emanated from their deceased husband, difficult. How much better it is to be able to sort out the finances whilst you are still around to do so. WRITE "ORGANISE FINANCE."

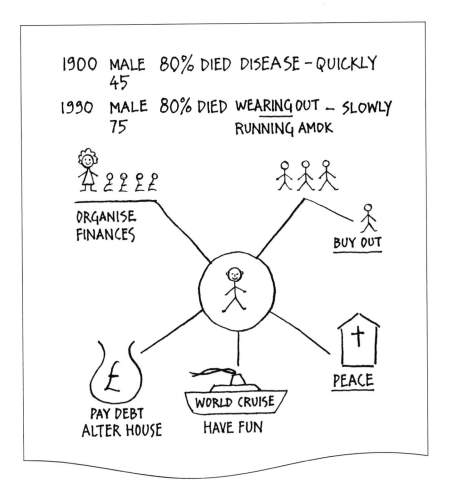

I continue

"You see, back in the nineteen hundreds, we developed the death insurance form of life insurance that served most family needs up until only perhaps ten or fifteen years ago. Life has now changed. What I have been talking about here is CRITICAL ILLNESS insurance which is proper LIFE ASSURANCE. You get the chance to sort your affairs out and look after yourself whilst you are alive."

I make the annotation on the A4 sheet.

The question then to ask is:

"What do I want to achieve financially?

Who do I want to achieve that with [do I need to financially cater for anyone else]?

How much money would it take to do it?"

and I write those three things down one under the other and then

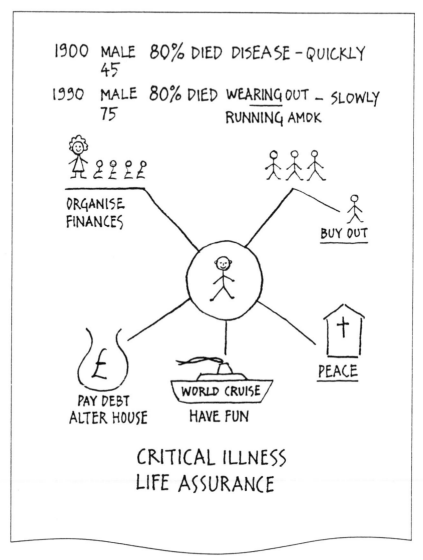

1900 MALE 80% DIED DISEASE - QUICKLY
45

1990 MALE 80% DIED WEARING OUT - SLOWLY
75 RUNNING AMOK

ORGANISE
FINANCES

BUY OUT

£

PAY DEBT
ALTER HOUSE

WORLD CRUISE

HAVE FUN

PEACE

CRITICAL ILLNESS
LIFE ASSURANCE

again looking straight at the client, I ask the question

"How much do you need?"

Responses are different on every occasion but I do find in my own environment that this is merely a preamble for me to say

" What I would really like to do is to present some figures for you to consider. Talk to your partners or fellow directors about the concept. Would that be agreeable to you?"

Most people actually say:

"yes we would like to see the figures"

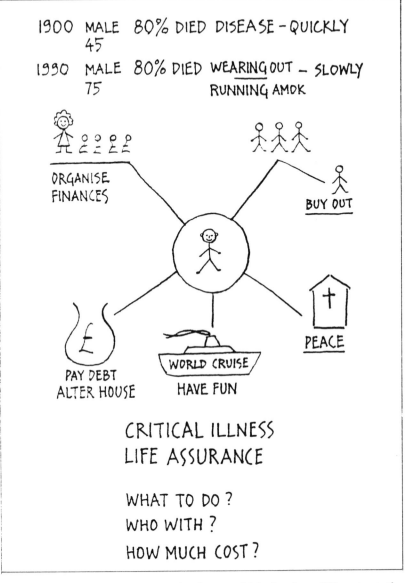

"What are your partner's dates of birth please?" - start the fact find proper.

"Do they work from this office?"

"What level of benefit should we talk about?"

"How does £100,000 sound, would that cover your requirements?"

and so on, and you are really into a professional interview.

Quill Mole

6

BE PROFESSIONAL, BE CONFIDENT, BE IN CONTROL

One has to recognise that other people are interested in their own problems - not yours. They are interested in you for what you can do to help them. That having been said, once you have asked the question, "How can I help you?", be quiet. Silence is golden; it really is. Be quiet. Silence demands a response.

Once you have established what it is that is required of you, and you know that you can help, then you can settle into your presentation.

I will still ask the question even though I perhaps have written before with a formal agenda, or a letter outlining our general services and some particular topics that I wish to discuss. I can follow straight in from their outline of what their question is to state that I require some information from them that will give me a background to their individual personal and/or corporate financial affairs. Then we can start looking at their actual situation.

"Do you mind if we spend a few minutes getting some details down, so that I can establish just how I might be able to put a solution together?"

The answer most assuredly will come "No, not at all." "What would you like to know?"

A basic fact-find doesn't vary very much at all. Most of us have our individual ways of working but we certainly need names, dates of birth, addresses, relatives, whether or not there are Wills, what investments there are, pensions, life assurance, unit trust holdings and so on. The company details, if they are relevant, turnover, profit, his and her earnings, other contributions to the household, investment income, rental income from property and so on.

Under no circumstances err or um and "it will be alright" IT WONT BE ALRIGHT - the client - the person with whom you are communicating will not GET YOUR BEST. YOUR BEST is what they deserve and should therefore have.

If they have the television on and make no move to switch it off, just say politely,

"Excuse me, please could we switch off the television as I find it affects my concentration. I want to give you my best and undivided attention."

AGENDA

Meeting to be held on Friday 13th
November, 1992
at 2.30pm
At the offices of Mole, Hill & Company
28 New Street
Anytown

Invited to be present:	G. Hill	N. Hill
	Z. Mound	A. Mole
	T.P. O'Halloran (Chairman)	

---

[1] **Apologies for absence**

[2] **Minutes of the last meeting [notes from last meeting]**

[3] **Points brought forward not covered in the agenda below**

[4] **Permanent Health Insurance**
     [a]*Self/spouse*

[5]   Life Assurance
[a]*Family protection*
[b]*School fees*
[c]*Special funds*

[6]   Pensions.

[7]   Items for future discussion

[8]   Date and time of next meeting.

Documents required at meeting, life assurance policies, pension policies, investment records, share certificates, stock valuation sheets, any other relevant financial data, memorandum and Articles of Association for the company.

A letter should be sent to the family confirming the date and time of the appointment and listing the items that are going to be discussed. A list of items that you wish to be available at that meeting should also be in the letter so that there is no fumbling about and rumaging in the attic. Birth and marriage certificates should be to hand, therefore, that should be noted in your letter or on your agenda.

Where house calls are being made, one should always endeavour to establish whether there are young children and at what time they normally go to bed. Make the appointment for after they have gone to bed.

Back in my 'family fun' days, I used to have an appointment at 5.00pm, 6.30pm, 8.00pm and 9.30pm every night, five days a week. My day time activity was administration, appointment making and developing a day-time job [seeing business clients and moving into the commercial market] together with attending college courses, seminars, insurance company presentations and so on.

Hey - if you are going to work; **go to work.** As John Savage says, life is not a rehearsal. This is it. You only get one crack at doing it right.

In a domestic environment I always assume control. If I do not have control - I leave. It is essential. We as life assurance professionals are set with the task of explaining an intangeable product and discussing a topic most people prefer not to talk about; their death. Control of the environment means eliminating competative forces like the television. If the householder says "shall I put the dog in the other room?" or "shall I turn the television off'' then say "thank you; that would be appreciated''

I have never had anyone refuse my request, actually that is not true. Sorry-I am prone to tell the odd white lie.

One evening I went to see a client in Brigg. I had an appointment and when I arrived the family were sat in front of the television watching a variety show. I asked if there was another room that we could go into and was told no; this was it.

I had travelled a long way, it was 9 o'clock at night I had no where else to go and there was a remote chance that I would get to talk business when the television programme had finished. On that one occasion I succumbed to the charm of the television and my host, sat back in the chair and was entertained.

Did I talk life insurance?　No.

Did I make a sale?　No.

Did I enjoy myself?　No.

When I left the house I was struck by abject remorse for having wasted one-and-a-half-hours of my time. I had failed a client by not insisting that we find somewhere that was quiet and private to discuss business or by establishing my professionalism by standing up and saying "you are obviously watching a very important programme and I don't wish to disturb that. I will give you a ring next week and make another appointment to meet you at your office. Will you be in on Tuesday, if I telephone you during the morning?''

You see had I done the professional thing, the client may well have recognised that he had invited me to his home to discuss business and, therefore, something should be done to make that possible. I have never fallen into the trap again.

Be professional, be confident, be in control.

If pets or children become a nuisance, again establish control "should I come back at some time when it is more convenient and I can just talk to you and your wife on your own?''

"What I have to say is very important, but what is more important, is that what you have to say to me requires my undivided attention, and I am afraid I cannot give you that whilst there are distractions in the room''. "How about if we make it a bit later in the evening?''

Hey gang? Don't back off. This is important, not for you but for the client. They have allowed you into their home to help them. You are letting them down if you try to do things second best. If you lose the sale you will gain a reputation. That I will guarantee.

After the meeting you will have established a lot of facts. You may well take documents away with you.

Always write and explain what you have done, note the documents that you have and what you are going to do with them, and establish a further contact date.

Note in your letter the topics that were mentioned during the meeting and who is responsible for getting further information or providing detail on each item. Is it them, their bank manager, their solicitor, accountant, you, the man next door, the building society, whatever, make the outline clear and precise using "paragraph and sub-set" as shown below:

Dear ......,

Thank you for your time on Friday morning when we discussed your personal financial affairs. I felt I should write and reiterate what was agreed:-

[a]   **We will establish the current level of life assurance available to you and then make recommendations concerning any proposed increases.**

[b]   **To establish the current position with regard to your home loan and the personal pension policy currently being used to provide surety**

[c]   **You will let us have sight of your own and your wife's birth certificates, together with your marriage certificate. These will be returned to you once we have made certified copies of them.**

[d]   **The various policies that I took away for scheduling will be returned to you within three days.**

Thank you for your instructions to act on your behalf. I will be in touch with you again shortly.

Yours.......

Probably the most important item in any letter outlining a course of action or a formal agenda is the term "complete documentation". Let you client know that this is where a formal application is going to be made or some documentation signed.

It may be that you are presenting a report, put that in and note the special features that are going to be discussed. Remember you never get a second change to make a first impression. Make the first impression count. People reward good business practise with good business.

Reports should endeavour to fit the personality of the client who is reading it and also, where appropriate, the financial or legal advisers that are working with them, but basically the report should fall into three parts. The **objective,** the **current situation** and the **recommendations.** (See Chapter 8)

Simplicity usually wins the day.

EFFICIENCY IN MEETINGS

How do you approach meetings with your clients? What impression do you give by the way you do things? Do you earn credibility by being professional in your approach?

There is a tendency to approach people to discuss their financial affairs, establish a need, produce a quotation and so on. The quotation gets sent off and then it is followed up with a telephone call and a meeting, the suggestions are taken up and we disappear - **forever.**

Lost opportunities using this "technique" are enormous; perhaps we can just discuss how matters can be simplified. Let me take an example.

I had a very successful director client. He had high earnings and capacity to provide full protection for his business and family whilst he also contributed at a reasonable level for his retirement.

A fair bit of planning had already been done when I came into contact with this man and I undertook a full report on a fee paying basis for him. The initial meeting was set up to explore various avenues, therefore, to ensure that we did not waste his time or ours, an agenda was formulated and he was notified in advance that we required certain documents and information.

That was standard procedure from our point of view, the personal assistant/secretary knew what to do and did it. I set the various items for the agenda and she had a set format as shown.

One should always list those people who are invited to attend the meeting so that they are clear that their presence is expected. This may include solicitor, accountant, company finance director, managing director, sales people or whoever is expected to provide an input. Always include yourself and any assistants or technical people that you are going to take to the meeting.

The first item on any agenda is **Apologies.** Having clearly stated, in the heading of the agenda the time date and venue for the meeting, plus the general topics for discussion, apologies should be listed on the agenda because the individual may wish to send in a written statement, even though they are unable to attend.

Minutes of the previous meeting. In my company we always produce minutes of important meetings and send them to all pertinent individuals. There may be items arising out of the minutes of the previous meeting that are relevant to our next set of discussions to which this agenda relates.

The body of the meeting then follows in the next three or may be four topics for discussion which may be, Permanent Health Insurance, Key-man Insurance, Partnership Insurance and Partners Pensions or Directors pensions.

By looking at the attached sample you will be able to adapt the format to suit your own particular requirements.

The penultimate item will be **Any Other Relevant Business** and invariably the last item is **Time and Date of Next Meeting.**

The agenda lends professionalism both before and during the meeting. It also provides a track to run on when doing the minutes after the meeting and is a useful tool to bring forward items which may be Item [3] and [4] on this agenda which time did not allow a full discussion and they can be brought forward to the next meeting.

Again, be professional and allocate time for the agenda to be gone through. If you only get up to item [3] or [4] on the agenda, then call a halt to the meeting, provide minutes and paperwork relating to what has gone on. The time and date of next meeting will bring you in where you left off. It will also bring you in with fresh minds for the topics under discussion and not overload the client.

Whoopee Mole

7

THE WONDER OF HOUSE PURCHASE

Why would anybody want a mortgage?

They want to buy a house; right? Of course they do. That is all they want to do, buy a house. However.....

If the people who want to buy a house can get an additional benefit at no extra cost, then they will do it. If the individuals concerned can get extra benefits with a higher degree of certainty, then they will be even more inclined towards that particular course of action . People have a variety of risk profiles and reasons for action.

I am rather conservative, a traditional with-profit type of individual and whilst I appreciate that you, the reader, may not be of that particular persuasion, I would ask you to be patient while I pour out my soul through the ink of this pen. To divulge for you the method that I use of taking people through the three main methods of repaying a mortgage.

Every mortgage repayment has three elements:-

a)   **The payment of interest on the outstanding capital. (Herein after called interest).**

b)   **The repayment of the capital at sometime in the future.(Herein after called capital).**

c)   **The repayment of the capital on premature death. (Herein after called life).**

| CAPITAL AND INTEREST SCHEDULE | | | GROSS PAYMENT |
| 10% INTEREST | | | 11418.34 P.A. |

YEAR	CAP.O/S	TOT.ANN.INT	CAP.REPAID	NET.PAYMENT
1	100000.00	10471.31	947.03	11418.34
2	99052.97	10372.14	1046.20	11418.34
3	98006.76	10262.59	1155.75	11418.34
4	96851.01	10141.57	1276.77	11418.34
5	95574.24	10007.87	1410.47	11418.34
6	94163.77	9860.18	1558.16	11418.34
7	92605.60	9697.02	1721.32	11418.34
8	90884.28	9516.77	1901.57	11418.34
9	88982.71	9317.65	2100.69	11418.34
10	86882.02	9097.68	2320.66	11418.34
11	84561.36	8854.68	2563.66	11418.34
12	81997.70	8586.23	2832.11	11418.34
13	79165.59	8289.67	3128.67	11418.34
14	76036.92	7962.06	3456.28	11418.34
15	72580.64	7600.14	3818.20	11418.34
16	68762.44	7200.33	4218.01	11418.34
17	64544.43	6758.65	4659.70	11418.34
18	59884.73	6270.71	5147.63	11418.34
19	54737.10	5713.69	5686.65	11418.34
20	49050.45	5136.22	6282.12	11418.34
21	42768.34	4478.40	6939.94	11418.34
22	35828.40	3751.70	7666.64	11418.34
23	28161.76	2984.90	8469.44	11418.34
24	19692.32	2062.04	9356.30	11418.34
25	10336.02	1082.32	10336.02	11418.34

"Tell me Mr Potts, have you ever had the various types of mortgage repayment methods explained to you in detail?

"No" is almost always the reply.

"Then let me explain them to you".

The most basic form of loan is the capital and interest repayment loan which I shall call a **repayment mortgage.**

Under the terms of this type of mortgage, the borrower [mortgagee] will repay to the lender. [the mortgagor] an amount of money each month which comprises interest on the capital outstanding and, as a proportion of the monthly payment is made, an ever increasing capital element. If tax relief is available, then it is usually available only in respect of the interest paid on the loan, not the capital.

The repayment mortgage is set up as shown in the following table. If we consider a mortgage loan of £100,000 over twenty five years, then the repayment schedule would look like those shown below. It does not take into account any form of Income Tax relief as that does not concern us for this purpose.

CAPITAL AND INTEREST SCHEDULE   **GROSS PAYMENT**
15% INTEREST   **16471.94 P.A.**

YEAR	CAP.O/S	TOT.ANN.INT	CAP.REPAID	NET.PAYMENT
1	100000.00	16065.45	396.49	16471.94
2	99603.51	16011.71	460.23	16471.94
3	99143.28	15937.73	534.21	16471.94
4	98609.06	15851.85	620.09	16471.94
5	97988.97	15752.17	719.78	16471.94
6	97269.19	15636.46	835.48	16471.94
7	96433.71	15502.15	969.79	16471.94
8	95463.92	15346.26	1125.69	16471.94
9	94338.23	15165.30	1306.65	16471.94
10	93031.59	14955.25	1516.70	16471.94
11	91514.89	14711.43	1760.51	16471.94
12	89754.38	14428.42	2043.52	16471.94
13	87710.85	14099.92	2372.03	16471.94
14	85338.83	13718.60	2753.34	16471.94
15	82585.48	13275.99	3195.96	16471.94
16	79389.53	12762.23	3709.72	16471.94
17	75679.81	12165.87	4306.07	16471.94
18	71373.74	11473.65	4998.29	16471.94
19	66375.44	10670.15	5801.79	16471.94
20	60573.65	9737.49	6734.46	16471.94
21	53839.19	8654.89	7817.05	16471.94
22	46022.14	7398.27	9073.68	16471.94
23	39648.46	5939.63	10532.31	16471.94
24	26416.15	4246.52	12225.43	16471.94
25	14190.72	2281.22	14190.72	16471.94

You can see from the table that at year five, hardly anything has been paid off the capital owing. You can also see by comparing tables [1] and [2] that an increase in interest rates from 10% under table [1] to 15% under table [2] results in a higher repayment figure and yet, even less having been paid off the mortgage at year five.

I then ask the question:

"How frequently do you think people move house in the United Kingdom?" They will come up with a couple of answers and I will tell them

"The average person in this country moves house every five years".

"If we look at the repayment schedule graphically, with the amount that we repay on the vertical axis and the number of years it is paid over on the horizontal axis, given a fair wind and level interest rates, the graph would look like this."

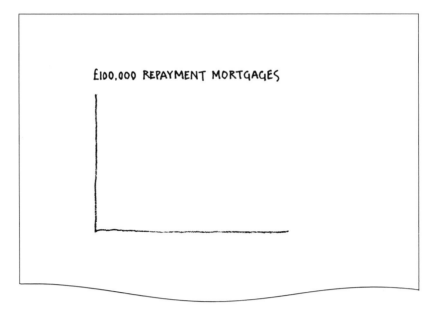

At this point I draw a straight line graph. A horizontal line at the bottom saying this is the period of the mortgage in years, and then a vertical line on the left-hand side and I say

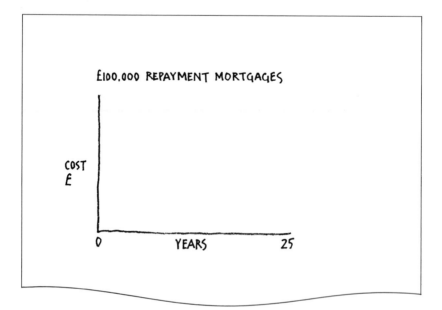

"This is the cost"
I write a pound sign and continue by saying

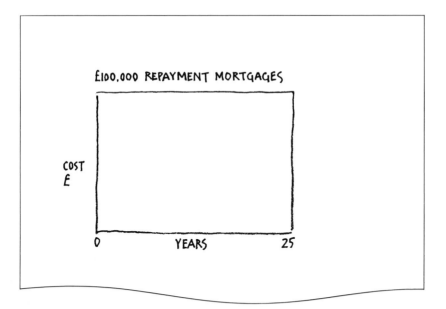

"If we assume constant interest rates, then our line for the graph looks like this"

And I take a line from the top of the vertical axis and move it across until we reach the twenty-five year mark and say

"Of course we could bring a vertical up to meet it which would complete a rectangle.

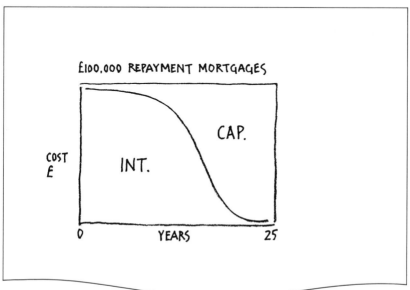

I then draw in the "S" configuration laid on its side which breaks up the interest and capital and label them INT and CAP.

"The reason for describing this graphically is to highlight the two component parts, interest and capital, but also to compare how the cheapest form of life insurance, a decreasing term assurance moulds itself into the profile of the outstanding capital. I was to draw the profile of that insurance then it would look like this".

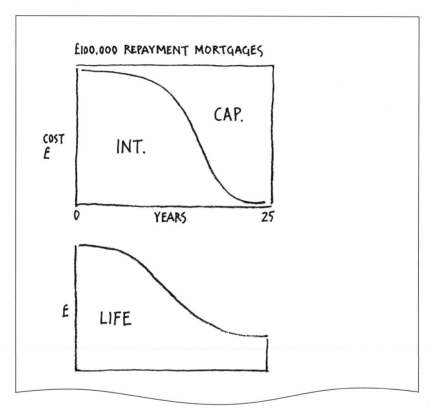

Next I would draw underneath the rectangle depicting capital and interest a further vertical line which is the cost of the insurance and a horizontal line which depicts the time and runs the same length as the original time scale of the repayment mortgage. I then draw in a similar "S" profile to show how the decreasing term tapers off as the mortgage progresses and capital is repaid.

"Most decreasing term assurance policies do take account of a variation in interest rates plus or minus 3%. They have to do this, as with varying interest rates, the amount of capital actually outstanding over time can vary considerably. Looking at these tables you can see why that is''.

At this point I may well refer back to the original 15% and 10% mortgage repayment tables just to show the client the difference in cost.

"There are two main alternatives. An interest only mortgage secured by a low cost endowment, or a pension mortgage which we will discuss later."

I then will say to them,

''Very few people relish the thought that there is no mechanism to discharge their mortgage at some stage in the future. therefore, I will ignore the interest only mortgage. We shall assume that you do require to redeem the mortgage at some stage and, of course, that you will want to discharge the mortgage should you (or "either of you") die before the due mortgage date. A full endowment mortgage provides a super deluxe method of linking an investment policy to a mortgage repayment. However, it is very expensive and you are, unnecessarily, locking your investments up with the purchase of a house.

A full endowment policy with profits, could double or even treble its "face" value over a twenty-five year period, dependant upon which life insurance company it is placed with. It will provide more than sufficient capital to discharge the mortgage liability with a lender and have substantial funds remaining for you."

The lender will normally require a policy at outset that has a death benefit equal to the loan [sum assured] A full premium endowment with a sum assured of £100,000 could mature with a pay out of as much as £300,000. The monthly premium would be £350 [or thereabouts] and all of the investment potential, the loan values and extra security would be tied up to that one domestic mortgage from outset. Some lenders will take bonus additions to the sum assured into consideration over time if a larger mortgage is required. In our considerations here I am saying that you retain a level mortgage over the full twenty-five year period even though you move house every five years.

A LOW COST ENDOWMENT — INTEREST ONLY MORTGAGE

In the early 1970s the Royal Insurance and the Provincial Building Society pioneered a scheme by which future bonus additions could

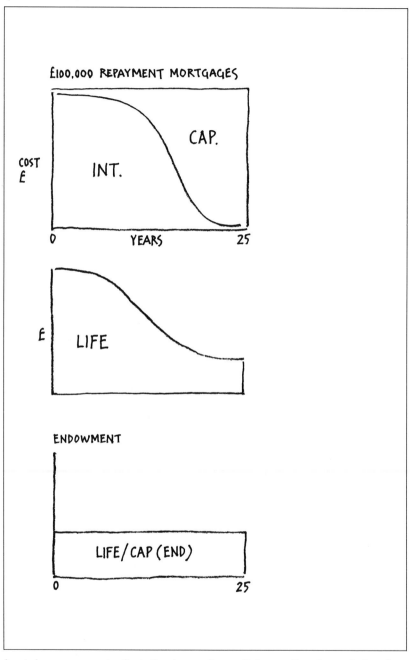

be taken account of at the inception of the policy by reinforcing the endowment sum assured at that point by a decreasing term assurance.

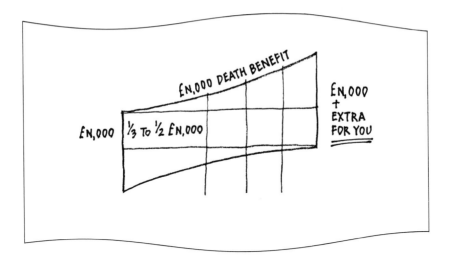

The decreasing term assurance would reduce at the approximate rate at which bonuses were anticipated to be added. By this means, the death benefit under the policy would remain "constant" over the full twenty-five year period of a mortgage and any additional bonuses at maturity would be payable to you [the borrower]. The premium for the endowment portion of an interest only endowment mortgage is considerably reduced.

At this point, and whilst I continue talking, I draw a long low oblong box and then I do a triangle on top to show the bonuses adding at the right-hand end, showing a substantial increase and then I extend the left-hand line down underneath the box and do a triangle underneath reducing: in that I put D.T.I. [decreasing term insurance]. I then draw two or three vertical lines down through the whole arrangement, then I will just add death benefit equals mortgage.

Now I may not use that every time in my mortgage presentation. Some people do understand low cost endowment. That is really only if they ask what a low cost endowment is and why can't we use a full endowment. If that question is not asked, then I go straight on to the alternative which is an endowment mortgage, using a low cost endowment which combines the cheapest form of insurance with the most expensive and we use that as a platform like this and, again, I draw an oblong and in this box I write LIFE/CAP and I tell them this

"All we have done is move the capital repayment from the building society down to this platform which, of course, is the insurance company''

I then draw the interest on the top with a gap in it for perhaps a period of time when there is no mortgage and therefore no interest paid.

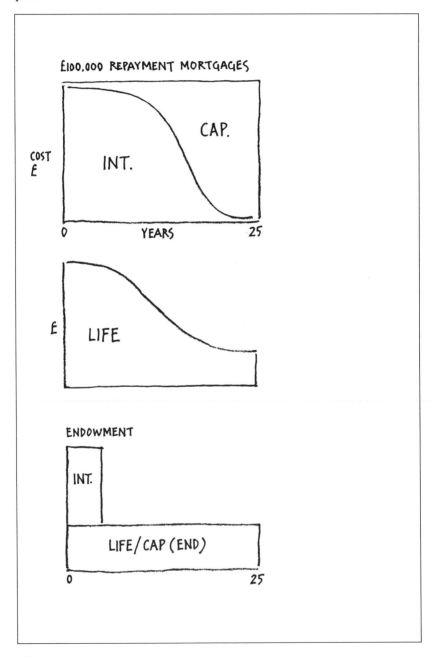

The result is that:

[a] The capital is repaid by the low cost endowment policy

[b] The life assurance is provided by the endowment assurance and the decreasing term assurance and maintained at the level of the mortgage over the whole twenty-five year period

[c] Interest only is paid to the lender.

The cost of this exercise is approximately equal to a repayment mortgage plus a mortgage protection assurance [another form of decreasing term assurance].

Flexibility

"Let us now compare what happens if we move house in five years time. The first house is sold and the second purchased. See how the interest paid to the first lender ceases and the endowment policies continue as the underlying platform for the next mortgage.

At this point you will draw an upright oblong box depicting interest payments above the horizontal box depicting the endowment and leave a gap between it and a second "interest" box.

A new lender, who perhaps has a cheaper rate of payment is chosen and interest is now paid to them until we discharge this particular mortgage. The continuity of life cover is complete - there is no further Underwriting to worry about and in essence five/twenty-fifths of the mortgage has been accumulated ready for the repayment date.

You should not even consider surrendering this particular policy at that juncture, even if you are not immediately going to take up another mortgage. The fact is that you may well take up another mortgage in the future and the loss to you in investment terms would be substantial. The only reason that I could see for the endowment to be cancelled at this stage, that is surrendered for a cash value, would be impending or actual bankruptcy. It is very difficult to find another investment source that can provide the level of return that even a low cost endowment provides at very low [virtually nil] risk.

On the basis that you move house every five years the endowment provides the capital and life assurance base for each successive mortgage until the end of the fifth mortgage at the twenty-five year term ORIGINALLY SET, WE HAVE SUFFICIENT FUNDS TO REPAY THE MORTGAGE AND AN ABUNDANCE LEFT OVER FOR OUR OWN PRIVATE USE, INVESTMENT OR WHATEVER.

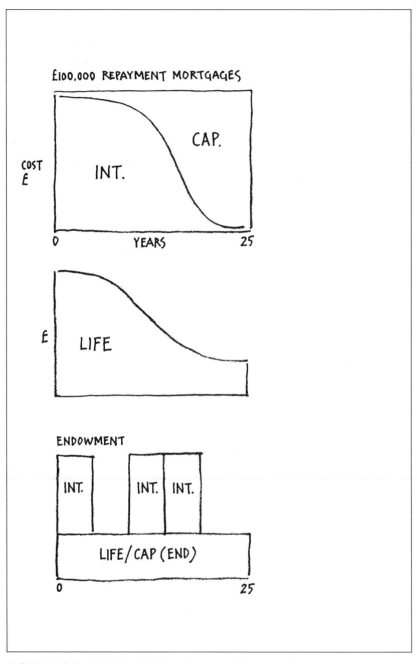

COST FOR COST THE REPAYMENT METHOD OF BOR-
ROWING AND REPAYING MONEY COMPARED TO THE
INTEREST ONLY - LOW COST ENDOWMENT METHOD - IS

NECK AND NECK. The argument for a low cost endowment mortgage is overwhelming in terms of the virtual certainty of an excess of funds and its flexibility when moving from house to house.

There is another facet of the low cost endowment mortgage that we should consider, and that is, of course, the non-mortgage. Suppose at the end of year five you take a job that either provides a house or you leave the country and, therefore, do not want to be encumbered with a property. By maintaining the low cost endowment assurance policy for, let us assume, a five year period - in between mortgages - you are still contributing to the final mortgage repayment if you re-enter the mortgage market at a later date. You can see from my diagram that the five years interest payment has been missed whilst an accumulation of capital for the future has been achieved.

Many people adopt the perception that a life assurance policy is inextricably linked to the particular mortgage that they have taken out. It is not. It is merely an assignment.

"Take a ten pound note and look at the front of it. It carries the name of a bank, and the facsimile of a signature of a man we have never heard of. When I give that to you in exchange for goods", at this point, I hand over a ten pound note, "I am assigning the right of that piece of paper to you. You in turn can get value for that piece of paper in money or money's worth".

"A policy of assurance is no different. It is issued by an assurance company and is also signed by a person we have never heard of. It is freely assignable from one person to another for money or money's worth to its face value. When your mortgage is discharged, the policy of assurance is merely assigned back to you just as certainly as if you had left a £10 deposit for the golf clubs at the Crazy Golf Course or a boat on the river. When you return the clubs or the boat, others re-assign your piece of paper with the name of the bank and the signature of the person you have never heard of, to the value of £10. The only difference is that the "numbers" on an endowment policy are a lot larger, but that should not intimidate you."

If I am discussing a pension mortgage I always complete the low cost endowment presentation and then compare **that** to the pension in cost and benefit terms

The presentation still fits into one A4 sheet with tax relief added as a tick against the three component parts - INTEREST, CAPITAL AND LIFE.

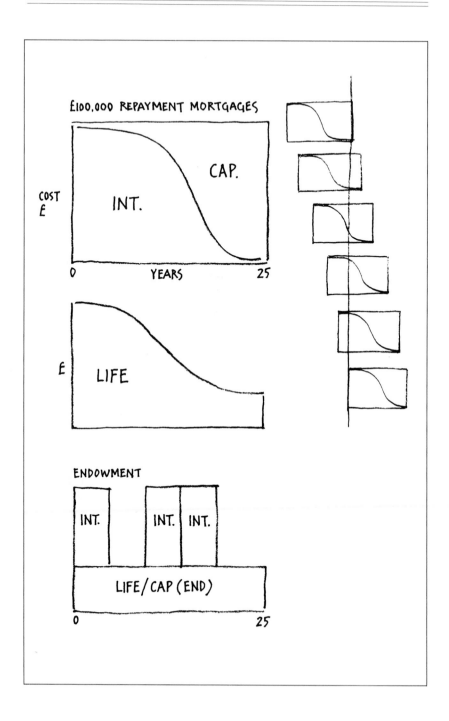

Domestic Mole

Case Study 1

James was a Flight Lieutenant at R.A.F. Scampton when I first met him, to give his financial affairs a thorough review. As it turned out I set up some whole life assurance, a small amount of Convertible Term and some Family Income Benefit to protect his daughter's interests. She was a dot of about six years old at that time.

I remember we avoided a flying risk extra loading which prevailed with most insurers at that time by using a specialist Underwriting Office.

However, there was an existing policy with Norwich Union. It was the only policy he had. Maureen, his wife, was not insured. The Norwich Union policy still had a couple of years of flying risk extra premium to pay until it reverted to normal rates.

The sum assured was £3,000 on a whole life non-profit policy basis.

A 'non-profit' policy simply means it had a guaranteed return, as I am sure you will appreciate, and I certainly had no hesitation in incorporating it in the general overall financial plan that we produced.

In 1970, when the Norwich Union policy was taken out, you could buy a three bedroomed detached house in the east of England for £2,300 [two thousand three hundred pounds.] This £3,000 policy would provide a house for Maureen plus a little bit to spare. My review took place in 1975.

In 1978 James and Maureen decided to buy their first house and obtained a mortgage of £14,100 which we arranged for them on an interest only basis. The surety to the building society was a Joint Life Low Cost Endowment of £11,100, premium £15.80 per month payable for twenty-five years, and a £3,000 Low Cost Endowment with Norwich Union which came about without any flying extra through the conversion of that £3,000 Whole Life Policy that I mentioned earlier. The premium - £3.20 per month.

Some time later James and Maureen moved away and we lost touch with them until 1988, although we did know that they had moved house again two years earlier. They had taken out a ManuLife Low Cost Endowment policy for £42,600 at a premium of £79.18 per month, which included the flying extra. Flying extra was usually payable for seven years as a fixed loading on the policy which varied with the rank of the individual effecting the policy. The lower the rank the higher the loading on the basis that one was dealing with a less experienced individual with probably a lot more flying to do.

In 1988, as I said, James and Maureen came back to me for advice and once again they were moving house and increasing their mortgage. This time they required an extra £8,000 which once more they sought to secure through an interest only mortgage by topping up the £8,000 over a further twenty-five year period, with a new low cost endowment policy; this time with Scottish Amicable at £13.67 per month.

The beauty of the whole scheme was that that original 1978 converted low cost endowment was still poodling along providing the bed-rock for the original twenty-five year policy and then that was gradually topped up as shown in the diagram below. To keep costs low, the terms of the successive new mortgage endowments were each extended to a further twenty-five years.

By 1991, a house extension was on the cards and £10,300 was required to fund that particular exercise with a top up from the mortgage, which incidentally by this time had moved through four different lenders. The General Accident provided the Low Cost Endowment Policy, and charged a premium of £21.30 per month for this top up Joint Life policy. General Accident also provided the new policy when James and Maureen added another £15,000 over a twenty-one year period [to stay in line with that 1988 policy] in February, 1992 at a further premium of £33.11. Yes this nomadic couple have bought a new home and moved on yet again.

It would have been nice to have got to 2002 and related the maturity story behind this case study to compare the results and see what a PEP mortgage would have done or a pension mortgage [which was not actually available to this client in his circumstances at the time] or even a re-payment mortgage.

What we can see from our vantage point at the time of writing is the flexibility of the Low Cost Endowment method of house purchase in terms of lender [a total of five different lenders now involved over the fourteen year period] and a strong possibility that in 2002 and on the subsequent maturity dates, there will be not only enough cash to pay off the mortgage, but a sizeable extra sum that will help to ease the way into early retirement: if that is what James and Maureen want. And **tax free** to boot.

Case Study 2 & 3

A quick contrast to the James and Maureen case study centres on Janet who we discussed in relation to the lack of Family Income Benefit and also to Jeff Brown a great friend of mine.

You may remember Janet's story and the untimely death of her forty-one year old lorry driver husband from a heart attack. [Chapter 2]

They did not have any Family Income Benefit insurance but they did have a Low Cost Endowment Mortgage which allowed Janet to pay off the mortgage and ensure that there was a roof over her head and the heads of her two daughters, for the foreseeable future. At the time of writing she still lives in the same house; rent and mortgage repayment free for over ten years.

Jeff? He was a flier. A pilot who came to me to organise his mortgage and Low Cost Endowment, again through converting his existing policies. He was buying a house and getting married about eight months later. All the preparations were under way, the conveyance went through, contracts were exchanged and tragically Jeff was killed when his fast jet flew into the side of a mountain.

His fiancée and his aging parents were released from the burden of having to sell that particular property, which would have had to have been sold in very difficult times, as the housing market was extremely 'flat' in the mid-seventies.

They were also spared the problems of their indebtedness increasing to the building society on a mortgage that would have been difficult to pay for a house that was not easy to sell. The debt could well have become more than the house was worth over the two or so years that it actually took for the market to improve. They were spared all that, by the 'miracle' of life insurance, through a Low Cost Endowment mortgage and a little touch of financial planning.

One Percent!

8

MR 'ONE PER-CENT'

It still surprises me, although I don't know why it should, that someone with a wife, children or perhaps elderly parents in the family borrow substantial sums of money from the bank on overdraft and then die leaving the unfortunate relatives to pick up the tab end of the debt.

It is hardly fair.

A PERSON'S DEBT SHOULD NEVER OUT LIVE THEM.

It is our duty as life assurance professional to give wide and vivid counsel to those people who would otherwise find themselves in this position. If you cannot convince the person who has actually got the debt, convince the people who are likely to suffer in the wake of the debt, and explain the simple principle of the self-cancelling loan.

The first thing I do during a fact find is to ask if the person has an outstanding mortgage, loan or overdraft and, of course, the result of a positive reply is to ask "is your indebtedness self cancelling on your death?" The usual reply is" I don't know"

My reply is "the chances are that it is not" "Let us have a look at what the interest rate on your particular loan might be and find out from the bank whether it will be cancelled on your death or not" Usually a simple 'phone call to the bank, building society or finance company concerned will establish whether the debt would pass to the family [or a business colleague] and if it does we can proceed.

"Which of the follow loans would you prefer to have?"
That is the question we ask and we immediately start writing on our A4 sheet of paper

A DEBT THAT PASSES TO OUR FAMILY ON DEATH

Then put a percentage rate in, and for the sake of the illustration we will use 13%

"Now Mr Smith we will call that a standard loan - your loan" and we write on the pad STANDARD LOAN - YOUR LOAN 13%

A DEBT THAT PASSES TO YOUR FAMILY ON DEATH

STANDARD LOAN - YOUR LOAN 13%

"now as we have said, if you die", and I write " Die" with a hyphen after it,"then your debt is still outstanding" and I write

A DEBT THAT PASSES TO YOUR FAMILY ON DEATH

STANDARD LOAN - YOUR LOAN 13%
DIE - DEBT STILL OUTSTANDING

DEBT STILL OUTSTANDING. "This means that your spouse or estate [children in the long term] have to pay the bank back", and I write down SPOUSE OR ESTATE [CHILDREN IN LONG TERM] HAS TO PAY BANK BACK

A DEBT THAT PASSES TO YOUR FAMILY ON DEATH
STANDARD LOAN - YOUR LOAN 13%
DIE - DEBT STILL OUTSTANDING
SPOUSE OR ESTATE (CHILDREN IN LONG TERM)
HAS TO PAY BANK BACK.

"Now there is an alternative loan, a self-cancelling loan, but of course the interest rate is slightly higher"

For the sake of this illustration, we will use 14%, therefore I would write on the piece of paper, having left a reasonable space, SELF CANCELLING LOAN - 14%

A DEBT THAT PASSES TO YOUR FAMILY ON DEATH
STANDARD LOAN - YOUR LOAN 13%
DIE - DEBT STILL OUTSTANDING
SPOUSE OR ESTATE (CHILDREN IN LONG TERM)
HAS TO PAY BANK BACK.

SELF CANCELLING LOAN - 14%

"In this instance if you die" and at this point I write DIE and a hyphen, "the debt is totally discharged" and I write DEBT TOTALLY DISCHARGED.

A DEBT THAT PASSES TO YOUR FAMILY ON DEATH

STANDARD LOAN - YOUR LOAN 13%
DIE - DEBT STILL OUTSTANDING

SPOUSE OR ESTATE (CHILDREN IN LONG TERM)
HAS TO PAY BANK BACK.

SELF CANCELLING LOAN - 14%
DIE- DEBT TOTALLY DISCHARGED

"This means that there are no worries for your loved ones" They have total security and I write down NO WORRIES FOR YOUR LOVED ONES. TOTAL SECURITY. Then I leave another space.

A DEBT THAT PASSES TO YOUR FAMILY ON DEATH

STANDARD LOAN - YOUR LOAN 13%
DIE - DEBT STILL OUTSTANDING

SPOUSE OR ESTATE (CHILDREN IN LONG TERM)
HAS TO PAY BANK BACK.

SELF CANCELLING LOAN - 14%
DIE- DEBT TOTALLY DISCHARGED

NO WORRIES FOR YOUR LOVED ONES,
TOTAL SECURITY.

"We can actually take the principle a little further. You will be well aware that a heart attack or cancer or some major disability can actually create just as big a problem, particularly in a business environment, if you have a major disability or suffer from a critical illness".

"If you had been given six or twelve months to live, would you want the loan or overdraft to be cancelled?" Invariably the answer would be "it depends; what it would cost?"

"A self-cancelling loan in this instance would probably cost 15%" and at this point I write down on my A4 sheet of paper SELF

A DEBT THAT PASSES TO YOUR FAMILY ON DEATH

STANDARD LOAN - YOUR LOAN 13%
DIE - DEBT STILL OUTSTANDING
SPOUSE OR ESTATE (CHILDREN IN LONG TERM)
HAS TO PAY BANK BACK.

SELF CANCELLING LOAN - 14%
DIE- DEBT TOTALLY DISCHARGED
NO WORRIES FOR YOUR LOVED ONES,
TOTAL SECURITY.

SELF CANCELLING LOAN - 15%
MAJOR DISABILITY OR DEATH

CANCELLING LOAN MAJOR DISABILITY OR DEATH 15% and then underneath that HEART ATTACK/CANCER - MAJOR DISABILITY DEBT IS SELF CANCELLING

It is then for us merely to beg the question, and I write it on the bottom of the A4 sheet "which loan agreement do you prefer?" I turn the paper towards them, put my pen on it, and let them think

A DEBT THAT PASSES TO YOUR FAMILY ON DEATH
STANDARD LOAN - YOUR LOAN 13%
DIE - DEBT STILL OUTSTANDING
SPOUSE OR ESTATE (CHILDREN IN LONG TERM)
HAS TO PAY BANK BACK.

SELF CANCELLING LOAN - 14%
DIE- DEBT TOTALLY DISCHARGED
NO WORRIES FOR YOUR LOVED ONES,
TOTAL SECURITY.

SELF CANCELLING LOAN - 15%
MAJOR DISABILITY OR DEATH

HEART ATTACK / CANCER - DISABILITY
DEBT SELF CANCELLING

WHICH LOAN AGREEMENT
DO YOU PREFER ?

it through for as long as they like without saying a word.

We all have to appreciate that any new concept that is put in front of a client, needs to be thought through before it is acted upon, and by giving them time to think, they can then make a rational, unpressurised decision.

Obviously, the concept presentation that we have just made, should be relatively acurate and, if anything, erring over the cost, rather than under. People appreciate honesty and if you can deliver more, by virtue of coming back with a slightly "lower interest rate" for the special package, then they will be over the moon.

Whilst we are on the subject of business loans, many people have overdraft and the banks quite honestly pin them down to pay so much a month to pay them off, or perhaps they end up as a permanent feature of the balance sheet because of an attitudinal precept that it is the normal part of the firm's trading scene.

If you can point out how much interest people are actually paying on overdrafts and high-light the fact that really there should be some mechanism for paying it back at the end of the day, it may be that the self-cancelling facility can be linked up to a full repayment facility via an endowment or maximum investment plan arrangement, perhaps even using existing contracts, thus establishing an even stronger bond with the person what you are endeavouring to help.

Again, I tend to use a one page presentation using the general principles that I outlined in Chapter [7] on mortgages.

Case Study 1

Stephen J Green, is a firm of professionals with three partners aged around thirty-six and two older partners in their mid to late fifties.

The younger partners were buying their way into the business.

As you will know, bank loans vary tremendously from overdrafts which are instantly recallable to fixed term loans over a set number of years. Most bank loans, however, fall into a standard definition category and are referred to as being "2 over base or 2.25 over base or 4 over base".

The expression "2 over base" merely means that if we took the base rate of that particular bank as published, and added 2% to it, that would be the rate of interest charged on that particular loan. In 1987 the bank's base rate was around 9%. In March 1991 the base was 13.25%. The partners took out a £90,000 loan facility in March, 1987 and in March, 1991 they took up a £75,000 facility and the following indicates the level

Case Study 1 (ctd)

of insurances implemented at that time and the percentage cost appropriate to the "over base" rate that we have discussed. You can see how small the impact is and how effective the argument is for using percentage rates rather than premiums.

In March, 1987 some Pension Term Insurance was set up at £30,000 for each of the three partners at premiums between [.27%] and [.28%] per month. In March, 1991, borrowings were increased; yet again to purchase part of one of the older partner's shares as he retired [a further £25,000: again using Pension Term Insurance to aged sixty-five [.54%] per month to [.56%]

The means of repaying the loan in both of these cases was through the three individuals' pension arrangements. They had not been contributing anything like their full quota to pension and were unlikely to do so for their own benefit, therefore, funding for cash in this way and obtaining tax relief into the bargain was very pertinent to their circumstances.

By 1992, the three of them had decided that although they needed to raise a further £20,000 each to look after the residue of a deceased partner's holding in the firm, they had used enough of their pension capability to that end and an alternative, therefore, had to be found.

A fifteen year low cost endowment was chosen to provide early repayment of the debt, [even though longer term figures were presented and advised] for the extra £20,000 each at premiums of around £67.00 per month. The life insurance element of the endowment would be approximately .6% of the loan.

The point that we are looking at in this case study is that the extra circa £85.00 per year, represented slightly over a quarter of one percent [.28%] to make the loan self-cancelling. By 1991, it had cost just over one half of one percent extra to make the loan self cancelling [.54%] and a similar proportion would apply to the insurance element of the Low Cost Endowment, used in March, 1992.

A self cancelling loan at an extra quarter or one half percent is a buying concept, not a selling one.

Case Study 2

The same is true of Edie. The numbers are small but they are still just as relevant.

Edie borrowed £18,000 to buy into a partnership and although she is single, there is no way that she would want her family to have to wait for things to settle to discharge her indebtedness to the bank in the event of her death.

A self cancelling loan at a cost of 0.31% per year extra is a cheap option to secure the peace of mind that she required. So that is the loan that she took. The self cancelling vehicle was a term insurance to aged sixty, written under pension term legislation.

At a cost of a third of one percent, gross, [yes before tax relief] it is a cheap option for a female just under forty to take.

Teacher Mole

9

DELIVERING YOUR MESSAGE EFFECTIVELY

To most of us writing a report is a bind, an inconvenience and a troublesome waste of time and effort. Reports certainly go against the 'single page concept' principle behind this particular publication.

For many clients, however, a report is a necessity - certainly for scrutiny of complex subject by other professional advisers perhaps.

A report should be delivered in similar vein to a single page rationale. Simplicity is the order of the day and again we come back to the client's current situation, the client's objectives, the alternatives and our recommendations.

So let us have a look at the structure of the ideal report. It was interesting to note in a personal survey carried out with several small groups of people that I presented them with an actual report with a transparent front cover and two empty file jackets, one a plain white gloss background with blue printing on the front and the other with a bottle green textured jacket and gold lettering on it. The question was quite simple; **which report do you prefer?**

Everybody, in each group questioned, without hesitation, chose the dark green empty jacket.

What we deduced from this is that visual impact is extremely important - in fact - most important.

"Now come on" you say, "how can that be the be all and end all of a report"

Well let us analyse the way people communicate and may be that will, in itself, illustrate fully the importance of presentation and visual impact.

Taking the total communication process as being 100%, I want you to visualise that I am stood in front of you now speaking these words to you and I will ask you this question.

"What proportion of this total communication [this message], is actually carried to you by the words?"

The actual words only communicate 7% of the total content of the message with most people. **SEVEN PER CENT**

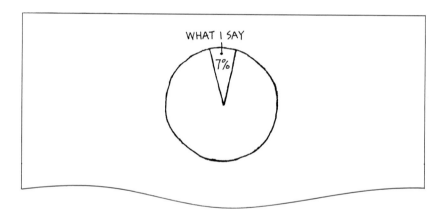

Now what about the tonality? How I say what I say?

Again using your imagination, and listening to my seductive tones, I might say

"Come here" in a very soft fluffy voice.

Alternatively, visualise me as the sergeant major, barking my communication across the parade square to some unfortunate "erk" who has stepped out of line

"Come 'ere!!"

That is tonality. How we say something.

What percentage of our total communication process would you say that takes up, of our remaining 93%?

38% is the answer.

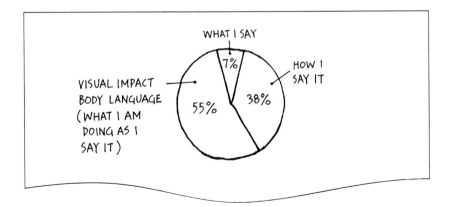

That leaves a massive 55% of total communication that is devoted to visual impact, body language [what I am doing, as I say what I say]

It does not take much visualising to see what would be going on in the body language sense when the words "come here" are being spoken in the two examples above.

In the first there would be dilated pupils probably open hands, maybe even beckoning. In the second the pupils would be narrow, firmly fixed and the body upright and authoritative. You would actually know what was going on in both sets of circumstances even you were behind a double glazed window just watching the scene without hearing any sound at all.

How does that affect report writing?

Well let us have a look at our pie chart again. What are the constituent parts of our written report.

Do we have words in a written report? - well most certainly we do, but do we have tone? Patently the answer is no. The only tone we have is the imputed tone which we place on the words in the context which they appear to us, and whilst the purist would argue that that would still come into our equation [and I would agree] for these purposes we must eliminate that from the discussion.

We definitely have visual impact. The report may have colour, dimension, form in lay-out and so on. What impact then does that have on the reader?

Now let us put a new pye chart up and see how the percentages change.

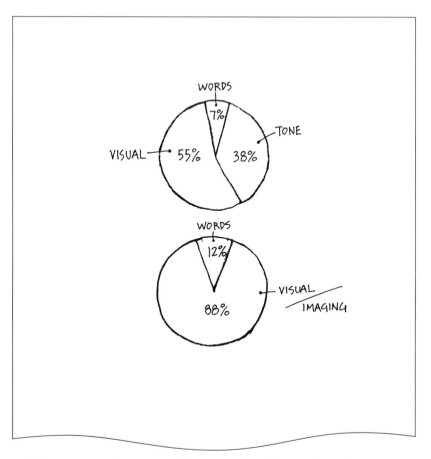

What we now have to do is proportion the words and the visual into 100% which is our non-verbal communication but the proportions will remain the same. Therefore of our new 100%, words will account for 11.25% which we will call 11% and the balance a massive 89% is visual impact.

Now we can see why 100% of the people who were asked which report they preferred, picked the empty cover. It was the most attractive cover, the contents of it were actually of secondary importance to that first impulse decision.

YOU NEVER GET A SECOND CHANCE TO MAKE A FIRST IMPRESSION.

You now know the reason why.

Having established that the visual impact of our report is

important. what can we do about it?

The first page of the report should always be a title and that invariably would incorporate the clients own name. People like nothing better than to see their own name in print on the front of a document, therefore your printed cover should have a "key-hole" title space in an appropriate position [probably two-thirds up the vertical face of the report cover, or if it is to be presented in a landscape format, two-thirds of the way up from the bottom of the landscape.] This gives natural balance and compliments the presentation. It also means that that page becomes the first page on your office copy, which gives you an internal report title without any addition work.

Always insert a blank sheet between the title page and the next page which is the index or agenda.

We shall be discussing agendas elsewhere in this book, but basically they provide a list of topics or actions for discussion, and could well be used instead of a simple index, which will merely give again the title of the topic under consideration and the pages on which the various "headings" can be found.

An index is particularly useful with a complex report. However,if it becomes a standard feature of **everything** that you do, then there is no danger that you would leave it out in circumstances where it could be important to the overall efficacy of your presentation.

In this age of word processors, it is also very easy to justify both left and right hand text margins, so that you get square and controlled form which looks disciplined and accurate, and gives credence to the words.

The next page will contain just one word; probably - "OBJECTIVES".

OBJECTIVES

The objectives should then be listed on the subsequent pages [usually one, possibly two in number in a bullet point format:

● to establish the continuity of the partnership in the event of a partner dying.

Bullet point two:

● to establish the continuity of the partnership in the event of a partner becoming seriously ill.

Next item:

● to examine the form of the partnership agreement...and so on.

A word of advice at this point is do not tackle too many topics at once.

Overload is the greatest source of procrastination. Two or three topics is quite sufficient unless you in some way prioritise segments of the report for future action.

Your next page will be a single heading "Current Position" or "Current Circumstances" or "Current Situation".

Never use the word "problem".

An outline of different circumstances in brief form will take up the next few pages with punchy paragraphs with plenty of space between them and "one and a half" or "two" times spacing between lines.

Double spacing gives the individual receiving the report space to read and also space for notes. The report is not just an inanimate heap of words. It is something that has to be acted upon and commented upon, therefore, we should make provision for that to happen within the document that we produce.

Our next header is "Alternatives" or "Alternative Solutions" In all sections one should keep the style punchy to enable the reader to sift their way through a fully justified and well spaced text. In this chapter, all of the alternatives should be explored briefly and discounted or supported as appropriate.

To use a simple example, if one was looking at a mortgage, then this particular section might discuss a re-payment mortgage, an endowment mortgage, a pension mortgage, a PEP mortgage, a mortgage linked to Unit Trusts and covered by a whole life policy and all of the alternatives that one can come up with these days as possible answers. The objective would be to make the most favoured alternative the penultimate in the discussion piece and the last item, either a lesser favoured and a discounted alternative, which in that case might be a PEP mortgage. We have to bring a little contention into the most mundane of topics.

RECOMMENDATIONS

What we want to look at now is the "recommendations" and that is our single word in the centre of our next page.

As with the "objectives", our **"recommendations"** should

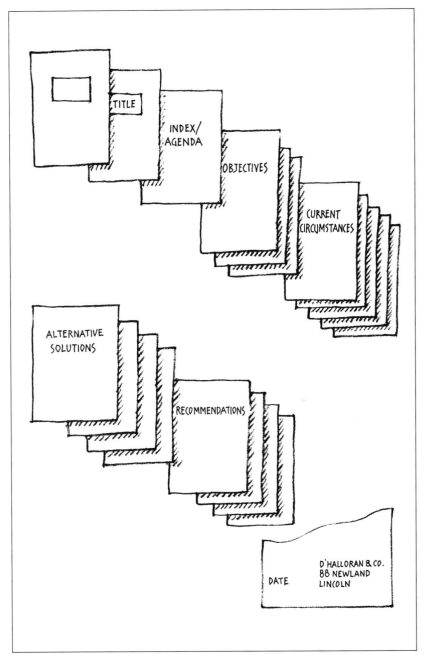

be succinct, clear and direct in their approach. In this way the client is left in no doubt as to which way we feel they should go. There may be one of two recommendations.

When we are looking at alternative solutions and recommendations, reference should be made to appendices that support the general views that are being put forward. The appendices follow on from the recommendations and may contain policy details, mortgage rates, comparisons, trust formats, wordings, whatever is appropriate.

Appendices should be clearly marked, well defined and well spaced out. I favour using broad computer paper for tabular recommendations. In that way they can be spread sideways. The computer paper actually gives its own authority to what is typed on it, whether it has come off a computer or not. One can fold the right hand end of the "landscape" presentation into the A4 format quite easily to be opened out as the report is read.

At the end of the recommendations, one should always finish off with the date at the bottom left hand side and your own or your company's name and the author's title at the right hand side.

To summarise then.

We know that visual impact is most important because it gives credence to the words. Good grammar is obviously essential, syntax [the way the words are linked together] is also important.

Justify left and right margins if you have word processing facilities, this is easy to achieve and looks more professional.

Be succinct, well spaced, authoritative and you will begin to enjoy the report writing process as your clients look first at the agenda, then at the list of "objectives" and then move straight on to your "recommendations", leaving the 'numbers' to those to whom it matters most.

ALL PRICES INCLUDE: FRENCH FRIED OR
BAKED POTATO, MUSHROOMS, PEAS,
ONION RINGS AND SIDE SALAD, SWEET
FROM THE TROLLEY AND ONE CUP OF
COFFEE (thereafter 50p per cup)

MEAT

PRIME FILLET STEAK	£10.55
PRIME FILLET STEAK	£10.95
WITH ANY OF THE FOLLOWING SAUCES	
Brandy & Mushroom Sauce	
or Green Peppercorn Sauce	
or Chive & Garlic Sauce	
or Tomato & Garlic Sauce	
SIRLOIN STEAK	£9.55
SIRLOIN STEAK	£9.95
with any of the above sauces	
PRIME FILLET STEAK	£10.95
Cooked to your liking with only a selection	
of salads from the salad bar	
FILLET OF BEEF	
STROGANOFF	£10.95
GRILLED CHICKEN BREAST	£8.95
Served with a tomato and tarragon sauce	
CHICKEN KEBAB	£8.95
Breast of chicken pieces with mushrooms,	
courgettes, tomato & peppers	
BREAST OF DUCKLING	£8.95
with Port & Orange Sauce	

FISH

GET STUFFED SOLE	£8.50
Fillet of Sole stuffed with Crab Meat, topped	
with parsley sauce	
or	
Stuffed with Shrimps & Garlic	
SCAMPI	£7.75
HOT SPICY PRAWNS	£8.50
& SCALLOPS	
Served in a spicy tomato & garlic sauce	

STIR FRY

A Choice of

CHICKEN & PRAWNS

or

SEAFOOD
Scallops, Prawns, Squid & Crab

or

DUCK BREASTS WITH
MUSHROOMS

All served with a selection of oriental stirfried
vegetables, rice and a spicy dip, sweet and coffee
£8.95

VEGETARIAN

VEGETARIAN LASAGNE	£7.25
NUT & MUSHROOM STIR FRY	
	£8.95

10

LIVE NOW —
PAY LATER

What do you do when somebody says to you they cannot afford life insurance?

"I cannot afford £50 per month for life insurance"

Remember that a lot of people think weekly. I very rarely use monthly premium illustrations. I talk to people in weekly terms, because if we say £50 per month, their brain automatically says "£50 a week that is a lot of money."

This applies as much to businessmen and directors as it does to employees.

If you talk to people about £12.50 a week, that is not quite such a problem. £12.50 a week, automatically registers in the brain, in the correct gender, for them to make a decision, and incidentally, £12.50 per week is £54.17 per month, which actually gives you 8% more premium to play with.

I have said it before: DO NOT CONFUSE ME WITH FACTS, IT IS WHAT I PERCEIVE THAT IS THE TRUTH.

The human brain works in the most contrary fashion. I am a factual person and I have had to work very hard at creating the style of presentation that people will accept; one that will move them to action.

If people still persist in saying that they cannot afford family life assurance cover, then I tell them

"I have to recommend you to 'Get Stuffed'!"

Sorry I am not being rude. "Get Stuffed" is a Lincolnshire Restaurant specialising in grilled steaks.

Now the thing is that most people go out for a meal at least once or twice a month, if not once or twice a week and if they came away spending £25 for the two of them for the evening's meal, they would feel quite pleased with themselves. Dependent upon what income level your potential client is at, so you might like to have a variety of menus from a reasonably cheap steak house like Get Stuffed to one of the higher quality hotels or restaurants in your area to illustrate the point that I am going to make.

I say to them

"Look here is the menu of one of the cheapest good quality steak houses in Lincolnshire, a meal for two will cost around £27.00 by the time you have had wine and a cup of coffee, possibly £30.00 to feed you for one day"

Tomorrow that one meal will be behind you - so to speak.

"what we are talking about with life insurance is £12.50 per week to feed your family for the next ten, fifteen, twenty years."

And then be quiet [your client will make his or her own decision. They will either take up the life assurance OR NOT.] It is their choice and mostly there is a positive response.

If they cannot afford the **premium** now, how are they going to survive without the life insurance money **AFTER** the **income producer or home maker** has died?

Happy Retirement

== 11 ==

WIFE'S PENSION

A one pager that I got some years ago from a Life Insurance Association meeting has served me very well. A tremendous amount of businesses are carried out by husband and wife teams who work together on a sole trader with the spouse as an employee principle. The avant garde sales person, or adviser, makes the observation that they are paying a fair bit of tax, why not effect a pension for the spouse.

"Well, er, we cannot afford it"

or

"Well, I want to put some thing away for myself"

or

"Not this year, maybe next year,

"Well, I cannot really see the benefits".

"I'll discuss it once we get the books done"

And of course, the books are always twelve to eighteen months late. By which time the opportunity has passed.

My one pager is quite simple. It explains a concept that puts the pension into perspective. The pension is unimportant, so therefore, put it out of the way.

"Tell me Mr smith, you employ your wife don't you?"

"Yes"

"Good, don't take her on as a partner whatever you do, because this little ruse won't be available to you if you do"

"What little ruse?"

"The one I am just about to show you. You will like this; not a lot.

Have you got ten minutes just for me to run through a little idea that I have got for you - it will save you a lot of tax"

"Well - if you insist"

"Let us say that you have a taxable income of £10,000, after your personal allowances and everything else, £10,000 TAXABLE income"

Then draw a picture of the client looking miserable with £10,000 underneath it, in figures.

"Do you agree Mr Client that you have to pay tax on that and let us say that that is 25%; £2,500 isn't it?

"err yes"

or even "How much tax do you pay?"

"err £2,500"

It is a lot better if they participate. The numbers sink in and they are involved.

"Now how much does that leave us with in your pocket?"

"£7,500"

"Fine"

In most marriages the system works this way.

What is yours, is your wife's

and

What is hers, is her own.

Is that how your marriage works?

A bit of humour, a bit of laughter and he says "Yes."

Fine. "How about if we give her what is hers now? I'll show you what I mean"

"Let's consider the same situation with you and £10,000 taxable income and your wife over here" and I draw a picture of her, and if she is present during the presentation it is even better. I would always get the wife there if possible. There she is a feminine looking match-stick lady with a frock and a smile.

"Now, of course, she is smiling because you are going to give her something, and what are you going to give her?....... £2,000, so let us put that under her,

and I put £2,000 below the lady's feet.

Now holding my pen down to the left of that I say, "now what does that leave in your hands? it's £8,000 isn't it?"

"Yes"

"Good"

I then write £8,000;

"Now what I am going to do is take £750.00 out of the £8,000 and put it over here in the box" which I then do.

"That leaves £7,250"

"Do you agree"

"Yes"

"If I take £7,250 and apply 25% tax to that, that amounts to?"

I then get my calculator out and work out the sum £7,250 x .25 which gives me a reading of £1812.50.

"Which leaves in your pocket?"

And I now take that amount from £7,250 and again put the amount on the paper.

"Now over here," [I have gone back to the left hand side of the page], "we have £7,500 in your hands after tax and that, of course, is to spend between the two of you".

If we add the £2,000 that your wife has plus the £5,437 that we have over here "[returning our attention to the right had working!]"

£10,000   £2,000
        £8,000
2,500   [£750]
_____
£7,500

"that means that we have put £750 in the box over here at a cost of £63 doesn't it?"

"Yes" the client should say.

"Is that good?" you remark.

"It depends upon what that £750 is doing."

I can then say "well that is accumulating over the next twenty years in a pension plan for your wife as an employee of the company. We do not have to work out 'her' contribution as a percentage of net relevant earnings."

I then show the result at the end of the day.

The surprising thing is that the individual is not interested in the amount of the pension. The only interest that I have ever had, and I have done this for lots for people, and presented full pension illustrations and what have you. The only thing that interests any of them is the fact that they are getting something for nothing. £750.00 in the box at a cost of £63.

Change their perception and do them some good.

Teacher Mole

Case Study 1

Wife's Pension

Robert is a cobbler. He has a little shop with modest workspace behind it, where he does his mending, soling and heeling. He has been repairing my shoes for a good few years and I have asked him several times whether he had thought about providing a pension for his wife, Linda.

"Not really" he said "You know I put the money away and I am as well putting it in my pension as hers, I get the tax relief"

He really did not want to talk about things too much because - well - his accountant did his pension and basically he was quite happy with what was being done.

One March I went in, after having seen this presentation at one of Clive Holmes "How" concept presentations in Solihull.

"Morning Robert" I said.

"Have you got ten minutes whilst I just show you something"

He was always game for a few minutes chat during the slacker part of the day, therefore, he ended up one side of the counter and I the other, so that he was on my right hand side. That is quite important - the same side as my pen. Linda was watching from a distance.

"This is you Robert" I said, and I drew my match stick man and followed that through;

I said,

"Is it right in your house, that what is yours is hers and what's Linda's is her own?" Linda chuckled.

I said. "Let me just draw a picture of Linda here" and I drew a super picture with curls and a bow and a big smile on her face.

I said - "You know why Linda is smiling don't you?"

He looked at me quizzically "because you are going to give her something"

Linda's eyes flashed and I said "£2,000 a year, watch this" and I put the £2,000 in.

When I had finished the presentation with the words......''and we have got £750 over here in the box.''

Robert said "Well, it looks like I'll have to have one of those, doesn't it?''

and he did.

As it happened the investment was only going to run for about six years until their joint retirement, [Robert is five years older than Linda] but, you know, we finally came to terms with what was in the box, because I went in to have some shoes repaired this year.

Linda asked the leading question: "Can I retire yet?''

"I don't know" says I.

"Well, can you have a look, because Robert is nearly sixty?''

"I'll put some figures together and I will show you them"

The figures are set out below

Robert had his own pension, which, as I said before, was organised through his accountant, but just look at what we have build up for Linda at a cost of £63 per year

Cost/Benefit Schedule

In 1985, investment income was taxed along with the husband's and a wife could only have earned income set against her own personal allowance. Things have changed now, but there is still a personal allowance to use up and we should not forget it.

In January, 1985, Robert put £750 in 'the box' for Linda. with a retirement date set at 1997.

Contributions continued at that rate until January, 1988 when Robert raised his employee wife's salary and her contributions to pension. That has been the regular premium ever since. There is room for more, but Robert did not want to do anymore. Instead he chose to top up with the occasional single premium:

    1989   £3,000   single premium
    1990   £1,000   single premium
    1992   £2,000   single premium

Now the couple have a dilemma [don't we all]. Robert, as I have said is five years older than Linda and he would also like to think he could retire at aged sixty. Now, if he does, then Linda would have an income of around £2,500 per annum for the rest of her life, ignoring a tax free cash sum and other relevant options.

If Robert works through until age sixty-five, Linda will, of course, be age sixty and her pension at that stage would be £3,800 per annum based upon current LAUTRO projections.

The net of tax cost of the whole exercise. Based upon moving part of Robert's income over to Linda and then putting first that £750 per annum rising to £1,000 p.a. into the box every year, has been, probably, less than £6,000. This has given Linda independence, security and the two of them the prospect of a better standard of living than they would have had in their joint retirement.

Linda will also be using her very valuable **personal allowance** with **earned** income.

Linda had been wittering on at me for a couple of weeks.

"Have you got those figures yet, have you got those figures? Can I retire yet, can I retire yet?"

My partner actually delivered the figures down to the shop and it was a couple of days later one lunch time when I went in and I was greeted by a broad grin and the simple statement.

"I can!!" and she giggled like a school girl. It really makes it all worthwhile.

Rich Git Mole

12

INTERESTING TAX RELIEF ON BORROWINGS

Qualifying loans are very important to people because it is only by having a qualifying loan that a business person can attract tax relief on loan interest.

A qualifying loan is basically money that is borrowed for a qualifying purpose which is normally "wholly and exclusively for the benefit of the business" concerned. Buying one's house is not a qualifying loan. Part of that loan may be eligible for MIRAS [Mortgage Interest Relief at Source], but the purchase of a domestic residence is certainly not "wholly and exclusively" for the benefit of a business.

Much as your mother, or possibly your grandmother, put money away on the mantle shelf in one of those magnificent tins that had wide slots in the top and five matching compartments underneath, that said rent, milk, electricity, gas and coal, the human brain tends to compartmentalise expenditure in an irrational and sometimes illogical way. The Inland Revenue have their music [the rules under which they operate] but we, by and large, are allowed to make up our own words, provided we do not disturb the overall song too dramatically.

If I have lost you I apologise. I will now return to the simplicity of the A4 sheet and the business of establishing qualifying loans in certain circumstances.

In this instance I believe that case histories can help to illustrate what we are trying to achieve.

Robert was a partner in a firm, comprising seven partners. He was a senior partner and had £70,000 capital in the firm, which was shown in the accounts under his "Capital Account".

Robert had children at private school and paid their fees out of his income, which of course was taxed as net profit. This was supplemented by an overdraft facility, provided by his kindly bank.

His overdraft when the fact finder was completed measured up to a substantial £37,000 upon which he was paying, let us say, 3% over base.

Robert also had a domestic mortgage of £30,000 [the MIRAS limit] on a domestic property valued conservatively at just under £200,000. The interest rate on the domestic mortgage was, say, 1% over bank base, less tax relief.

Robert had substantial pension contributions but was still paying a fair amount of tax. His problem was cash flow and capital funding for his partnership.

Robert needed £20,000 capital for the partnership.

Where to start? That was the question.

Well the first thing I did not like was the fact that there was a £37,000 overdraft with no tax relief, whilst there was personal tax paid cash sitting in the partnership Capital Account. If Robert had borrowed money from the bank to fund the partnership, because he had increased his drawings, full tax relief at the highest rate of tax applicable would have been allowed. That would have improved his cash flow tremendously.

There was a lot of equity in the domestic residence and also in the partnership property but in this instance there was also some unsecured money available at a reasonable rate of interest because Robert is a professional person.

"Robert", I said, "the first thing we have to do is get rid of that overdraft".

"How?".

"We will take £37,000 out of the business account and pay it off" I said

He gulped and went ashen, "but the reason I have got you here" he said "is that our bank is already pressing us to reduce our overdraft and we need more money in, not money out"

"Trust me" I said

"We are going on a tax efficient cash merry-go-round that will put everything neatly in its place and get you the tax relief that you are entitled to because, to be quite honest, you have been quite silly"

"Silly, why?"

"You have been building up this overdraft against school fees whilst you have been leaving your own capital, which is in effect tax paid income, or profit, whichever way you want to term it, in the firm"

"Well, I needed to do that because the firm needed the capital"

"But if the firm had borrowed it you would have had tax relief on the interest, so let us see if we can re-arrange it now so that that is the case".

Case Study 1

"The first step Robert, is to take £37,000 from the £70,000 capital account and pay off this overdraft and we will need to do that through the partnership trading account."

"I know that will push you into overdraft or further into overdraft, but let us follow it all through logically"

This is where the A4 sheet of paper comes in. I draw an oblong box a third of the way down the page on the left hand side about two or three inches in, and write at the top PTNRS.ACCOUNTS.

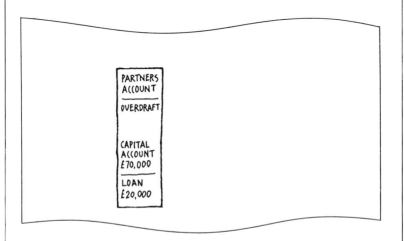

Below that I draw a line and write OVERDRAFT I draw another line about half way down the oblong box and under that I put CAPITAL ACCOUNT £70,000 I draw a line underneath that and I put LOAN £20,000 and that is the bottom box in the oblong. I then take a line out of the CAPITAL ACCOUNT £70,000 box and draw it up to Robert and put the number [1] next to it and I write to the right-hand side **'withdraw £37,000 capital'.**

I then draw a line from Robert to the bank which is an oblong box towards the top left-hand corner of the page, which says

REPAY OVERDRAFT £37,000 and I label that [2], this indicates that Robert has now personally paid off his overdraft.

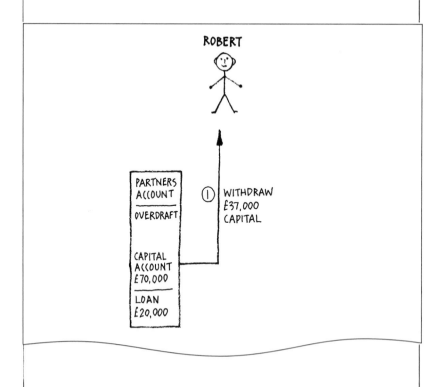

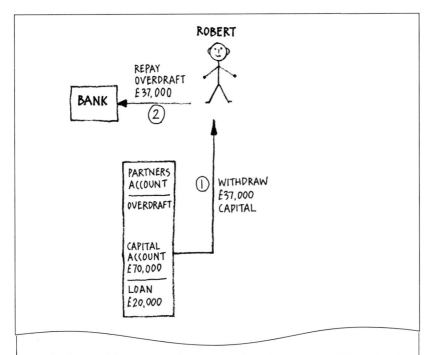

"The problem now of course is that the partnership is short of capital and therefore the partnership has to borrow from the bank to make up that deficit [3]. That is all well and good but, in fact, we would not wish to fund the school fees or the firm by means of an overdraft ideally because it is essentially core borrowing."

"Now Robert, I have said that we do not want to fund this on an overdraft; really it is not very satisfactory as the facility can be withdrawn at any moment at the whim of your bank manager, therefore, let us have a proper loan set up that will not only fund the amount that you have now taken out of the firm but also the £20,000 extra borrowing that you want to inject into the firm.

I have negotiated a £57,000 facility with a mortgage company to provide you with capital over a fifteen year period at 1% over base and we can get tax relief on all of the interest because it is a qualifying loan. £57,000 is injected into the partnership which puts the Capital Account back up to £70,000 plus the £20,000 introduced - £90,000 total. The £57,000 is a personal debt to you which in this case was unsecured but however, could have been secured as an extra mortgage on the house. We can repay the £37,000 that was temporarily provided by the bank whilst the loan was arranged.

I now draw a line down from the bank to the overdraft box in my vertical oblong partners account £37,000 [3]. Over to the right-hand side I draw a picture of Robert's house and I draw a box below that and in it I write

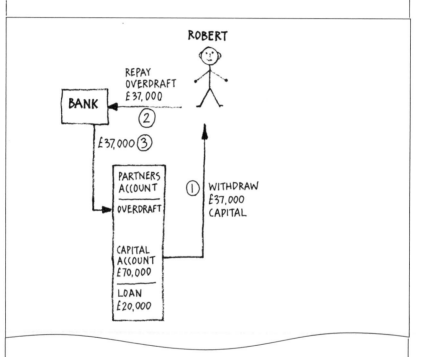

MORTGAGE COMPANY and I draw a line from that to Robert and then another line from the mortgage company straight down to loan £20,000 at the bottom of the heap and against that line I write £57,000 mortgage loan and I itemise that [4] and I split the loan at the bottom between the Capital Account and that Loan Account of £20,000, draw a line up from the Capital Account £70,000 to the Bank Re-pay Overdraft £37,000 and put [5] and that completes the arrangement.

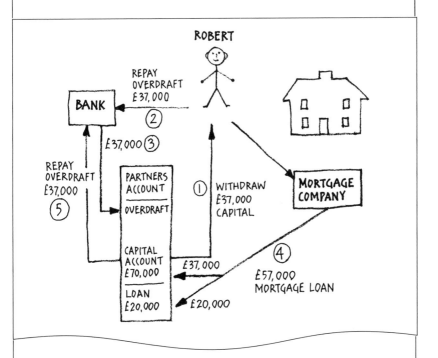

Then underneath my diagram I list out the summary which I am going to go through with Robert.

"So let us summarise what we have done. The first thing we have done is discharge the non-tax relievable personal overdraft of £37,000 by withdrawing that amount of money from the Capital Account.

The second thing we have done is arrange short term finance to make up the deficit within the trading partnership.

The third thing we have done is organised a proper commercial mortgage over a reasonable period of time, in this case fifteen years, for the amount of the overdraft plus £20,000 extra capital which we wanted to inject into the firm."

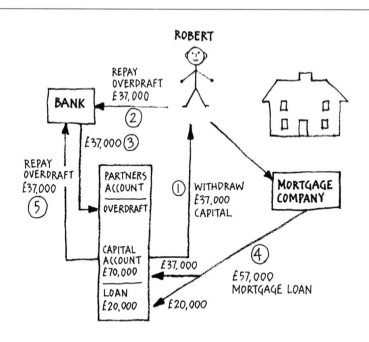

1. DISCHARGED NON TAX RELIEVABLE PERSONAL OVERDRAFT £37,000 FROM YOUR CAPITAL ACCOUNT.

2. SHORT TERM FINANCE OF £37,000 ON PARTNERSHIP ACCOUNT FROM BANK.

3. ARRANGE PROPER MORTGAGE OVER SUITABLE PERIOD TO REPAY PARTNER'S OVERDRAFT (CAPITAL INJECTION) PLUS £20,000 REQUIRED FOR CAPITAL IN FIRM.

4. PAY BACK BANK OVERDRAFT - RETURN TO STATUS QUO - SAVINGS ON INTEREST RATE.

Case Study 2

This case study is slightly different and therefore worth going
through because Chris was looking to buy a house.
He wanted a £60,000 mortgage.
He was paying higher rate tax.
He was having to leave substantial taxed profits in the
partnership with his father to fund expansion and again. The
A4 sheet of paper simplified the procedure so that he could
buy his house and get full tax relief on a qualifying loan to
the business. A domestic mortgage would have denied him that
apart from MIRAS on the first £30,000 of the mortgage.

"Now Chris, here is your set of accounts" and I again drew
an oblong box with OVERDRAFT at the top LOAN in the
centre and CAPITAL at the bottom to depict the accounts.

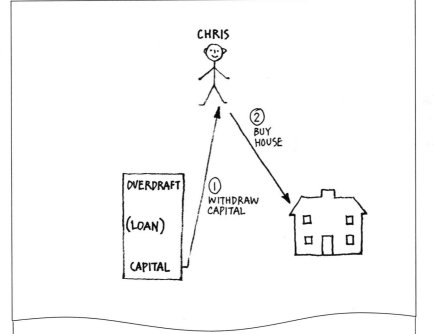

"The first thing you need to do is withdraw the capital from
the firm"
His response was
"But we need every penny that we have got in there at the
moment, we are expanding very fast"

"O.K, well let us see where we go from here because when we have withdrawn the money from the firm you are going to buy a house with it. It is your personal money, you have paid tax on it and therefore, you are entitled to use it for your own private purposes"

"Now having taken the money out of the Company, we have to get it back in again, so we will borrow on the business overdraft, hopefully not for too long, the £60,000 that we are now short of as working capital within the firm"

I then draw the bank and draw the overdraft coming out of the bank.

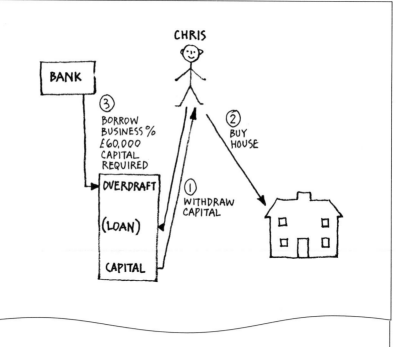

"So far so good. Now what we have to do is to borrow sufficient money on a long term basis to fund the firm properly and make sure that the core borrowing which we have now introduced is repaid at some future date. What we will do is approach a building society and, using your house as security, we will take up a mortgage and that will become a personal loan from you to the firm as capital introduced."

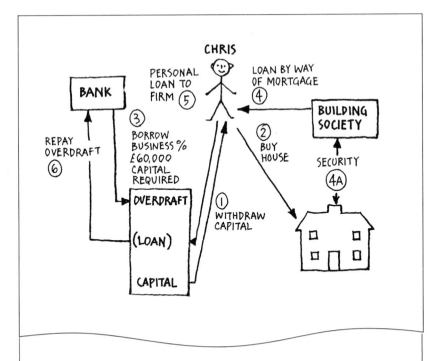

and I write in LOAN BY WAY OF MORTGAGE and PERSONAL LOAN TO THE FIRM and number those four and five respectively. So we have now put the £60,000 back into the firm, which will allow the overdraft to be repaid to the bank and then I summarise the situation to Chris just as I had done to Robert.

"So to summarise Chris, what we have done is [and I write this down on my A4 sheet]

1. **We have purchased the house with the tax paid capital from the firm's Capital Account**

2. **We have made up the shortfall in the firm's capital base by borrowing on an overdraft from the bank, itself a qualifying loan**

3. **A qualifying loan is available from a building society or bank on a personal basis which would include MIRAS and that capital would, of course, be paid to the firm who would then pay the bank overdraft.**

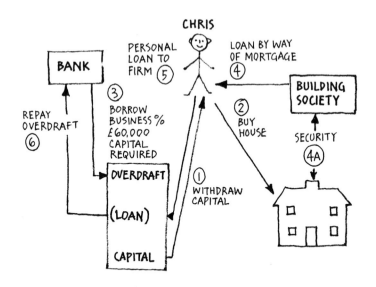

1. PURCHASE HOUSE WITH TAX PAID CAPITAL FROM FIRM'S CAPITAL ACCOUNT.

2. MAKE UP SHORTFALL IN FIRM'S CAPITAL BASE BY BORROWING ON OVERDRAFT FROM THE BANK.

3. QUALIFYING LOAN AVAILABLE FROM B. SOCIETY TO CHRIS (INCLUDING MIRAS RELIEF).

4. REPAY THE BANK OVERDRAFT.

Artesan Mole

13

THE SELF-FUNDING PENSION

Back in the days when Income Tax rates were 60% you could virtually arrange a pension for somebody for free. That somebody had to be self-employed, had to be a higher rate tax payer and had to be over aged fifty. They also had to be able to understand complicated tax legislation if you went about explaining the proposition in long hand.

These single page A4 presentations are not designed to do anything other than highlight the actual reason for doing a particular investment.

At the end of the 60% tax payer era I attended a Life Insurance Association [L.I.A.] regional meeting and this gem of a sales idea dropped into my lap. In fact most of these ideas came from speakers at the Life Insurance Association or local Life and Pensions gatherings, together with, of course, the major industry conferences. There is very little that is actually new. It was early February and we had until April to pick up on the previous years' tax rate to get it set-off against the second half tax payment due on July lst. I have to assume that you, the reader, understand the basic tax structure.

The typical client was aged over fifty, had a large tax bill due to be paid in July, having paid a substantial amount on January lst, and was paying 60% tax. Now whilst 60% tax rates no longer apply in the U.K., I feel it is worth illustrating what was available then, what is available now and by that token you can see what might be available in the future, and how to deal with it.

£20,000

On the left-hand side of the sheet I write £20,000 and I say to the individual,

"Let's put £20,000 into your pension fund."

"But I have not got £20,000 to spare, I have got this huge tax bill to pay, and what about my cash flow?"

"I can understand you position. However, the effect on your cash flow will be temporary. I can assure you that the results will be quite positive".

and then I go on.

"Here is £20,000 invested and you are paying tax at 60%, we can, therefore, get a tax claw back of £12,000 against your £20,000 premium, all hopefully deducted from the lst July payment. Do you agree?"

£20,000   £ 12,000
                 £ 4,714

A dubious nod may be the only indication of an answer.

I do appreciate that this is not always the way the Inland Revenue like things to be done but "needs must as the devil rides", so they say.

"Now on top of that, because you are over fifty, you can actually take your benefits".

"You mean I have to stop work?" is the usual response from seventy to eighty percent of the subjects of this presentation.

"No, no - you have to 'nominally' retire, which means that you ask the insurance company to pay you a pension and, of course, with the pension goes a 25% tax free cash sum with a nominal deduction for expenses. Let's say that they pay you £4714''.

£20,000   £ 12,000
                 £ 4,714
                 £ 16,714

£3,286   NETT TRANSFER
         TO PENSION A/c

INCOME £1580 P.A.

(£1185 NETT 25%)

"The balance of the 'pension fund' is actually paid to you on an annual basis for the rest of your life''.

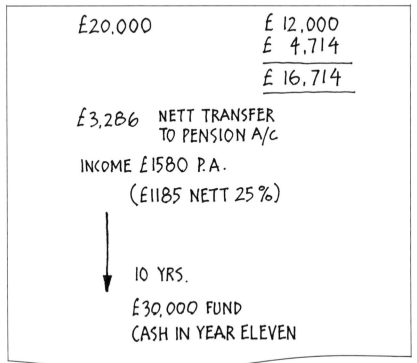

£20,000   £ 12,000
                 £ 4,714
                 £ 16,714

£3,286   NETT TRANSFER
         TO PENSION A/c

INCOME £1580 P.A.

(£1185 NETT 25%)

10 YRS.

£30,000 FUND
CASH IN YEAR ELEVEN

"Unfortunately that is going to exacerbate your current tax position. What we need to do is to take the pension back out of your income again and invest it, for say ten years time, when you actually retire.

There you have it, a self funding pension scheme which at age sixty will produce a substantial tax free cash sum plus an income to go on top of the original income".

£20.000   £ 12,000
                 £ 4.714
                 ─────────
                 £ 16,714

£3,286 NETT TRANSFER
        TO PENSION A/c

INCOME £1580 P.A.

(£1185 NETT 25%)

↓ 10 YRS.

£30,000 FUND

CASH IN YEAR ELEVEN

£7,500 TAX FREE

£2,250 TAXABLE ($^{10\%}_{\text{ANNUITY RATE}}$)

£3,830 P.A. FOR LIFE

GUARANTEED 10 YEARS

"The premium will be paid gross but of course will be eligible for tax relief which will directly offset the extra 'income' that has been generated by the 'pension' that you are drawing.

These contracts are particularly viable when annuity rates are high, or when you expect interest rates to fall substantially''.

One word of caution when using these contracts; the tax relief aspect has to be monitored carefully to ensure that the client gets everything that is originally promised. Watch out for overkill, especially with regard to loss of tax relief on that part of income that is the 'personal allowance'. You cannot get the tax relief for people where tax is not being paid [or is not eligible for payment].

Let's look at the current tax situation

An up to date example might be with regard to a 40% tax payer.

''You pay tax at 40%, therefore, you will attract tax relief of £8,000 which we will put in just here''

I write in £8,000 TAX RELIEF [40%] on the right hand side of my A4 sheet.

£20,000   £8,000 TAX RELIEF (40%)
               £4,700 25% TAX FREE CASH

NETT COST   £12,700
£7,300

''I said you could retire straight away and in about three weeks time you should receive a tax free cash sum of approximately £4,700. That represents your 25% of the fund tax free cash''

I write under the £8,000 ''£4,700'' and to the side of it ''25% tax free cash''.

I then total up the tax relief and the tax free cash to £12,700. Then, over on the left hand side I write NET COST ''£7,300'' and underline it twice.

"Now having 'retired' and taken the £4,700 tax free cash sum you are left with an income of £1,580 per annum which is usually paid to you net of standard rate tax. Because that is taxable income, what you need to do if you are not going to have that whittled down to £952.00 net of higher rate tax, is to put that amount back into a pension over the next ten years. That would generate a fund in the order of £30,000 in ten years time.

On the A4 sheet we can now write INCOME "£1,580 per annum" and put the net of higher rate tax and the net payable figures to the right hand side of that - short arrow down towards about the middle of the page and write "TEN YEARS" next to it and then "FUND £30,000."

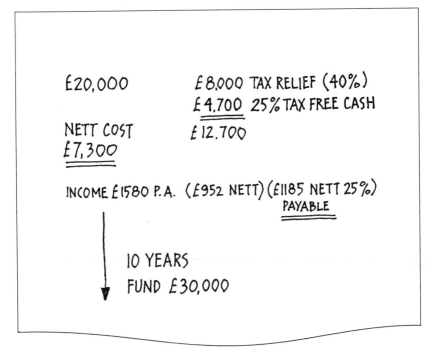

Just below the centre of the page and about two inches in I write CASH IN YEAR ELEVEN.

"When we get to year eleven you get another tax free cash sum and strangely enough that is about equal to the original net cost of the scheme so in effect now you have now had all your money back."

"In addition to that you also get another income, around £2,250 which is taxable [that is based on a 10% annuity rate]."

By this time I have written down '£7,500 tax free' and just underneath that "£2,250 taxable [10% annuity rate]"

At the start of the bottom quarter of the page about an inch and a half in from the left hand side I write "£3,830 per annum taxable for life - guaranteed ten years", and I finish off my presentation

£20,000   £8,000 TAX RELIEF (40%)
                 £4,700 25% TAX FREE CASH

NETT COST   £ 12.700
£7,300

INCOME £1580 P.A. (£952 NETT) (£1185 NETT 25%)
                                    PAYABLE

        10 YEARS
        FUND £30,000

CASH IN YEAR ELEVEN
        £7,500 TAX FREE
        £2,250 TAXABLE (10% ANNUITY RATE)

£3,830 P.A. TAXABLE FOR LIFE
        GUARANTEED 10 YEARS

"Now taking our original income of £1,580 which is no longer being paid to a pension plan, plus our £2,250 which is being paid out of the second pension [grossed up of course because these would normally be paid net of standard rate tax] you have a total taxable income, at no cost, of £3,830 per annum for life with a guarantee of at least ten years payments if you live or die.

I will admit that the mechanics of it can be a little bit messy and that one has to be very watchful of administrative errors, that tax is reclaimed on time, that the accountant is happy that your client deducts the premium relief from the July payment of tax and that the client does not mind paying a gross premium into pension when in fact they are only receiving the net of standard rate tax premium into their bank account.

For all of its potential complexity, the simplicity of the A4 presentation, coupled with your expert knowledge of your products, and the rules and regulations surrounding it, will lead to some very useful business and an excellent service for those clients who act on your recommendation.

The first time I used this presentation was just after attending an L.I.A. meeting one February and my thanks go to whoever mentioned the idea and sent me off with about six weeks to go to the end of the tax year.

I cannot remember precisely what the circumstances were, but I remember that the 60% tax bracket had been removed a year earlier and this was the last year that one could actually go back into that year to pick up the 60% relief. After 5th April, that was it, it had gone - forever.

Now the essence of the thing was that you had to have people who were aged fifty or over at the correct time. The criterion was that they were at least fifty years of age in the tax year under consideration.

So, I am running around like a demented hen assembling the names, addresses and 'phone numbers of all the people that I could think of who would be fifty or over, and I ended up with quite a number. One of them was Albert.

Case Study 1

Albert was a farmer and I knew that he was fairly profitable. I had known him for a long time and he was somebody that I could talk to.

"Hi Albert - how are you?" I said over the telephone.

"It's Terry, can you spare me ten minutes, I have an idea that will enable you to claw back a large slice of your 60%

---

tax and provide you with a free pension, can I come and talk to you about it?"

An appointment was made

Albert and his wife, Mary, worked very closely together in their farming business. They also run a couple of other little enterprises. I arrived at the door for the appointed time. Mary ushered me in.

After a brief bit ot chit chat, we sat down around the kitchen table to talk business. I went right through the presentation; - "Now here you are Albert putting in £20,000 to a pension scheme. Bearing in mind that this is February, you will feel the real benefit of getting your £12,000 tax relief back in July, when you don't have to pay that huge tax bill that is pinned up on your 'memo board'."

"Whilst we have got to wait until July to get your tax back in effect, you will, of course, retire in three weeks time and that will give you approximately £4,700 back as a tax free cash sum [that is 25% of the total fund which is the £20,000 that you put in less setting up costs]."

"The effect of those two cash sums coming back to you amounting to £16,700 means that the current cash flow outlay is £3,300 at say lst July when that tax payment is due. That is your total net cost. You are also going to get back £1,500 per year in income, but, of course, that will be added back to your current income which will create a further tax liability.

What we need to do with that, because you are not using your full pension entitlement at the moment, and as far as I understand it, you are not intending to use any of your existing income to increase pension contributions, is to take that £1,500 per year and roll that back through a new pension scheme for the next ten years. At the end of the ten years, here is your £3,300 back as a tax free cash sum from the new contract, plus a bit extra, let us say £7,500 and, of course, you have got your existing income which continues until your death and an extra income of £2,250 approximately per annum, which means that for the rest of your life you have £3,830 per annum with £2,250 of that guaranteed for at least ten years. That is assuming a 10% annuity rate of course."

"Here you are Albert, here is your cost free pension.

"Wow!" They were gob smacked.

I said,"the only criteria you need for this particular plan

is that you are a tax payer at the highest rate and that you are over fifty"

It was at this point that one of my most embarrassing moments occurred because Albert looked me straight in the eye and said,   "but I'm only forty seven"

If the floor could have opened I would have jumped in.

"Oh - I am sorry, I seem to have got it a round my neck don't I. I mean you could still do it but you would have to wait three years to retire"

I somehow talked my way out of it.

Then came those words which saved my bacon and presented an excellent opportunity to do some good, "But Mary is aged fifty and she is a higher rate tax payer, because she is a partner in the business"

He saved my life "We can do one for her can't we?"

The end product of this presentation was a very successful £7,500 investment - the tax relief was £4,500 plus the tax free cash sum of £1,712.50.

Albert is just about ready to do his now [1992]. The nice thing is that the tax relief comes out of the lst July tax payment so they can actually see the saving that they make, which had a much greater impact than the current method of paying premiums net, for employed folk.

A very satisfying exercise.

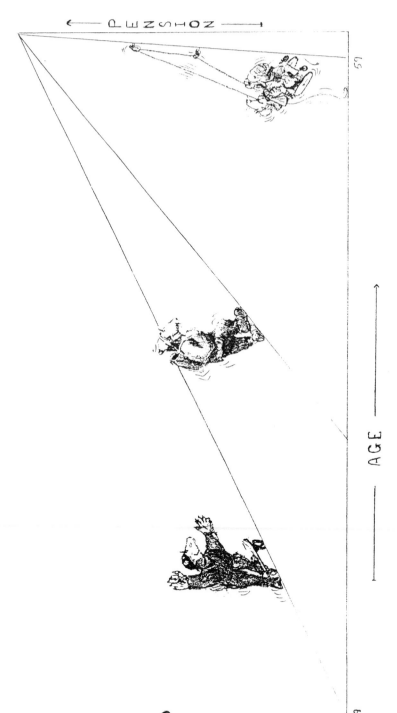

The Pension Graph

14

TRIANGLES

There are several one page presentations whichI have used over the years that lend themselves not only to a one to one presentation but also to group situations - the 'triangle' is one of them.

I cannot remember where the idea came from but I am certain it was somewhere on the Life Insurance Association circuit, or the National Convention. Wherever it came from, it has been refined to fit my own personality and style. I believe it creates a vivid picture in the mind of the recipient of the message as to the real values, costs and benefits surrounding their pension programme.

As with everything else, the presentation starts with "Here you are today" a dot about half way down this A4 sheet of paper marks the starting point. I write TODAY under the dot.

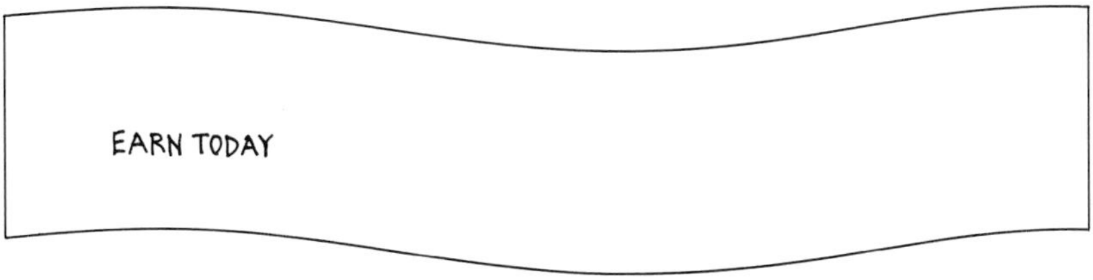

EARN TODAY

"How much are you earning"?.

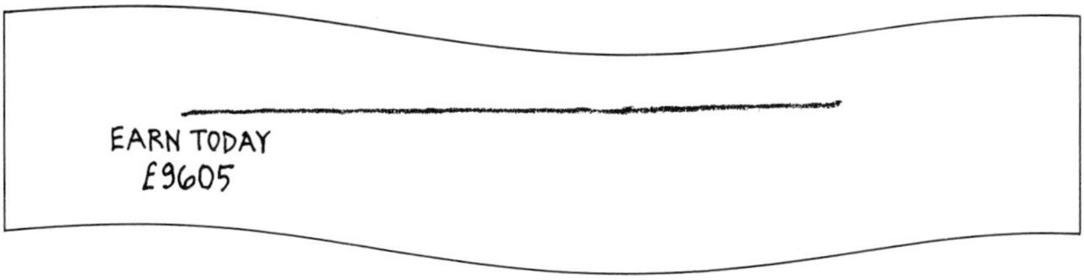

EARN TODAY
£9605

"Well, if we assume that this is your life line, then at this point, which we will call aged 65 for the moment, you will retire. Now with promotions, job changes, status changes and what have you, your income from now until retirement will probably go up by about 10% per annum, compound."

I now draw the slope of the triangle and then join up its back bone from where I have written 65 to the apex and I write RETIRE and the expected earnings at 10% roll up to that date.

Note:

Now there is an interesting rule that applies here, and that is the rule of seven. We have said that there is a 10% increase in salary, therefore, every seven years, the present day salary will double. Therefore, if you take the number of years from now until

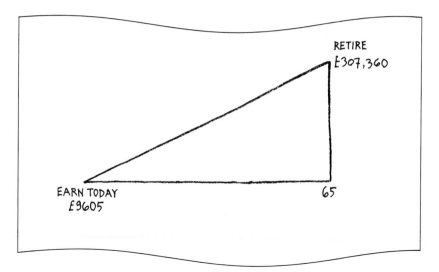

retirement, divide it by seven, then that is the number of doubling up functions that you have to do for an approximate answer.

This means that if we are talking to a thirty year old, we have to double up five times. So, taking our calculator we would put in £9,605 x 2 = £19,210 then we would multiply that by 2 which is our second doubler £38,420, then we would multiply that by two, £76,840 which is our third doubler, then we would multiply that by two, £153,680 which is our fourth doubler and then we would multiply that by 2 which is our fifth calculation, giving a final salary of £307,360.

There is an easier way of doing the calculation if your calculator has a "constant" facility on it, and that is to put in 2 times times and then put in the £9,605 = and then if you do equals a further four times you should come up with £307,360 - try it.

To return to our presentation then.

We now have a triangle, with today £9,605 on the bottom left hand corner, retire £307,360 at the top and 65 the retirement on the bottom right hand corner of the triangle, as shown opposite.

What I then say is "there are certain target incomes that we work towards in retirement, what would yours be in relation to the £9,605 that you are earning today?" and I leave it for the person themself to answer, but I may just put a helping hand in by way of "How much per week do you need to live on?" Then I remain silent.

You will have seen from a previous chapter that I believe people think weekly. I don't think, I know from experience that that is the way the majority of people's minds work.

By asking for the weekly amount that the person needs to live on, you will get a more accurate answer that is relevant to their circumstances as they see them. I believe that to be quite important. If there is too much delay, or indecision, then I may well use the phrase "most company schemes aim for two-thirds of current salary, would that be somewhere near your figures, about £115 per week and I put in the figure, [or two-thirds.]

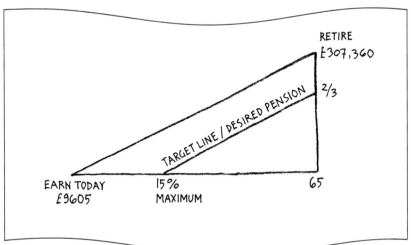

Note:
If it is a company pension scheme member we are talking to then the maximum pension is two-thirds final salary in any event and that would therefore go up the vertical line in the appropriate place.

Along the bottom line of our triangle, about a third of the way in from the left hand side, I would then write 15% maximum, [or in the case of a personal pension scheme, 17.5% maximum. Older ages will obviously be treated to higher figures as appropriate], and I join the two dots with a line and I write on the line "target line", or "desired pension".

I next establish how much pension contribution they are actually making at the present time, and if possible [in the case of a review] the amount of pension benefit they are actually buying at the moment. I put the amount of pension they are buying at the moment up the vertical spine of the triangle, and along the bottom, as near to proportion as I can get it without losing the clarity, I would write "4.5% of earnings" then underneath that the actual amount in weekly terms to bring it into the person's own perspective.

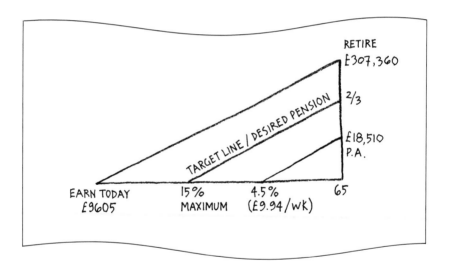

Many people do not understand percentages, they are confused by them. They can actually work against the sales process if the context is not appropriate.

The next task is to see what pension will be paid at 65 from the arrangement that is currently in force, reduce that down to a weekly payment in today's terms, and write in "at retirement you can expect to receive £12.94 . in today's terms" and, of course, we get £12.94 per week by working back arithmetically in exactly the same way as we work forward to get the future value of today's earnings.

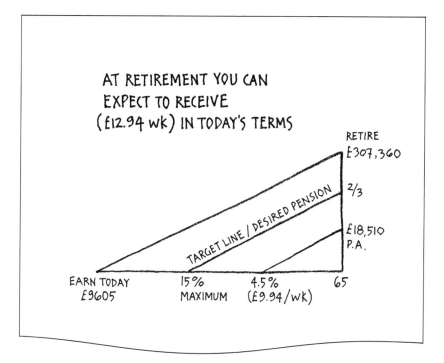

AT RETIREMENT YOU CAN
EXPECT TO RECEIVE
(£12.94 wk) IN TODAY'S TERMS

RETIRE
£307,360

TARGET LINE / DESIRED PENSION

2/3

£18,510
P.A.

EARN TODAY   15%   4.5%   65
£9605   MAXIMUM   (£9.94/wk)

I ONLY SAID THAT THESE PRESENTATIONS ARE SUPPOSED TO BE EASY FOR CLIENT, WE HAVE TO WORK AT THEM TO GET THEM INTO OUR MIND, TO ACTUALLY USE THEM. OUR CLIENT IS SUITABLY IMPRESSED BY OUR USE OF A CALCULATOR OR POCKET COMPUTER. THE POCKET COMPUTER OR A FINANCIAL CALCULATOR IS MORE ACCURATE,

However, a simple calculator even without a memory function should be an adequate tool given a little bit of practice.

All of our figures would be supported by insurance company produced figures under LAUTRO rules as applicable before a client did anything. However, this methodology does allow the **concept** to be put over in relatively accurate terms without misleading anybody, but rather putting them in a position where they can understand the quantum of the pension that they are purchasing.

On our review document we now add the last piece. I say, and write, [or have pre-written] underneath the triangle, "you need to put in an extra ...% of earnings to achieve two-thirds of your expected earnings at retirement, as a pension, amounting to the equivalent of £123.76 per week today.

Under that

Your State Pension will be £46.00 per week in addition to the scheme pension, in today terms.

Then I ask the question.....

"Could you live on £169.76 per week in retirement?"

It is just a matter of getting quotations to establish a premium that will provide for the short-fall between today's projected figures and the "amount" required.

What we can also do is to mark off on the right hand side of the diagram the percentage of salary that we are actually generating and that is achieved by dividing the prospective pension being purchased by the earnings at retirement. That will give us [@ 13% growth] 14.5% of salary that we are actually generating.

It is easy enough also to use a triangle as a method of showing people the increased difficulty that they will have in achieving their target, the nearer to retirement they get, before placing extra money into their pension scheme.

The logic is undeniable once a client sees how easy it is to walk up a shallow slope compared to climb up a precipitous rock face.

I think I should give an explanation of the rule of seventy-two which works as follows:

Take 72 and divide it by the amount per cent to get the number of years over which the principal will double; at that percentage rate. For example if we took 12% then 72 divided by 12 = 6 which is six years to double, WRITE THE PRINCIPLE DOWN IN YOUR DIARY NOW!

The rule of seventy-two.

Take the number seventy-two and divide it by the amount per cent that you wish to assume in your calculations and the answer will be the number of years over which, at that percentage rate growth, the amount will double, or at that percentage rate inflation, the number of years for the principal to halve.

We have seen, in the example in this chapter, a rate of 10% growth results in the principal doubling over 7.2 years.

7.2% interest would double the principal over ten years.

What about 4%. 72 divided by 4 = 18, therefore, at 4% the principal will double over eighteen years. Similarly at 18% inflation, the principal will halve in real terms over 4 years. [which is why inflation has to be controlled.]

Spender Mole

15

BACKING THE INVESTMENT MIRACLE

Everybody knows what they want from an investment. Security, a good return and, of course, capital to spend in the future should they require it. What they don't know, but think they do, is how to achieve it. Building society accounts, bank deposits and National Savings all produce income and all "guarantee" the capital. But what level of income do they guarantee? What level of income do they provide? By and large it is arbitrary and fluctuates with the market. It is the opposite of the Gilt market where the income is constant and the capital fluctuates, however, that is another topic.

I had extreme difficulty in convincing people that they should enter into an annuity contract, retain part of the income in an investment which would return the capital at the end of a given period [say ten or fifteen years] but in the meantime pay to them a modest net fixed income.

The reason for the difficulty was quite simple. Whatever the market interest rates are at any time reflect in the level of the annuity which one might obtain from a capital sum invested. Therefore, re-investing any part of that income for the longer term, gave a poor illustration of what income was available NOW.

After long and tedious conversations some people eventually saw the point and did take up the scheme on offer. All too often, the real point of the exercise was lost in a haze of verbal gymnastics.

The result from a building society investment was clearly shown, one would get 16% or 12% or 8.25%, no matter that some of that was compound annualised return [C.A.R.]. That is what the investor sees, therefore, it is fact. Remember "don't confuse me with facts, it is what I perceive that is the truth".

The standard quotation from an annuity backed investment would show the gross annuity being paid into the clients bank account, an amount being retained for an endowment and then the income that was available to the investor 7.1% instead of 10.25%. The brain automatically says 10.25% is better, I will stick with the building society because today is today and tomorrow, for some unknown reason, can take care of itself.

My dilemma was compounded because a lot of the people that I spoke to actually relied on income and were going to be in dire straights when interest rates fell; they would then have to dip into capital to support their life style. As they dip into capital, the income from the interest reduces even further so they draw more capital and so it goes on.

There had to be a way to put this onto an A4 sheet of paper and illustrate the point. There had to be - and there was. There always is. In this case it just took a long time to find it.

The illustration, and therefore the presentation, went together very easily indeed because of course the key to the whole argument is INFLATION. The impediment; the thing that was stopping folk investing in the annuity backed investment was the fixed portion that was "kept back" for the ongoing investment.

On past performance, we know that the investment should return a 5% - 6% compound return on the whole of the original capital invested at the end of a ten year period [based upon a ten year endowment policy maturing today] Because that was the proceeds of an endowment policy, a qualifying life assurance, the proceeds would be tax free.

If 6% of the investment return was being retained in the Back to Back arrangement this way, then surely that was the "inflation proofing" portion of the investment return and we should therefore, in comparing it with a building society or bank deposit, retain a similar amount.

And so the perspective was changed. My first task was to discuss the building society or bank deposit that the client had. When people rely on capital to produce income, they need to retain the capital, therefore, the tying up of capital for ten years is not an argument against Back to Back arrangements. The capital would be in the building society in ten years time anyway because they **need it** to produce their income from the interest earned.

I write down "building society 8.25% net."

Now what do we think the rate of inflation is going to be over the next ten years? Do you think 5% would be reasonable?

"Yes" comes the reply.

Good - let's put 5% of this 8.25% return that you get from the building society away for inflation. We will leave that in the account to accumulate. How much does that leave us?

8.25%

B. SOC.

5%   INFLATION

Most people are mathematically minded enough to be able to come up with 3.25% at this stage in the proceedings and I put that in underneath the 5% and next to it I write "to spend".

On the right-hand side of the sheet of paper I write at the top of the page "Back to Back arrangement" and invariably the person that I am talking to says "What is a Back to Back.?"

"Well, it is an annuity funding an endowment. That sounds very complicated but basically you are buying income and we are using part of it to put into an investment to return your income plus interest at the end of ten years whilst paying you an income throughout the period net of tax."

"Oh!"

"Don't worry about it, it is the concept that I really want to look at at the moment. We can go into the detail later [and we must of course]."

"If we look at the left-hand side of the page and your building society, we have set aside 5% of the interest earned on your investment and we are accumulating that compound, over the period of time that the investment runs. Do you agree?"

8.25%
B. SOC.

5%   INFLATION

3.25%   TO SPEND

"Yes"

"Fine - well, we will put 5% in here then" and I put that in underneath Back to Back and against inflation. The income that we can provide is 6.5% net and that can be paid monthly, quarterly, half-yearly or yearly, which would you prefer?" "Well, I get my building society interest monthly." "Fine - now can you see that you are getting 3.25% over here with the building society and 6.5% here from the Back to Back arrangement. At this stage we usually have some favourable comment; but I move on.

8.25%   BACK TO
B. SOC.   BACK

5%   INFLATION   5%

3.25%   TO SPEND   6.5%

Now, if we take a look at the building society again, what would happen if interest rates went down to 7.25% net? Would we still have to retain the same 5% for inflation, well yes I suppose we would and that would leave us how much to spend? 2.25%? that is right, 2.25%. If we look at the Back to Back arrangement, because we have bought into an annuity which is a fixed income over the full ten year period, you are still getting the 6.5% net that we originally started with.

The product is the same, the end result is the same as that which we had outlined in long drawn out, mind blowing, technical conversation that I had when I was first putting these things together for clients.

Now it is on one piece of paper, easily illustrated and the person can see the benefits in the correct perspective. Their perception has been altered sufficiently to take up the investment.

Case Study 1

It is amazing how many people think that Trusts can only be used for Family Income Benefit policies and Inheritance Tax planning. They are a lot more versatile than that.

Frank received a legacy when his father died that produced a capital sum of around £160,000. Frank wanted to release himself from his main business, such that he was not dependent upon it for income. However, he did have other business interests which produced a reasonable standard of living and he was currently paying higher rate tax.

Margaret, Frank's wife, had a very modest income of £2,400 from the business, although she did work quite hard in her capacity as book-keeper, varnisher and odd-jobber. The thing is that there was a National Insurance downside of paying her more.

If we could invest the capital and Margaret could have the income, then this 'emancipated woman' could use her own personal tax allowance for unearned income and together they would get the joint benefit without any National Insurance problems.

Most men would be reluctant to give away £120,000 so that their wife could have earnings below the higher rate tax threshold and Frank was no exception.

"What does your milkman look like?" I asked Frank, and we all laughed.

"Have you thought of a Back to Back?" I asked, and we went through the presentation and then I added a little bit to it.

"You can see that Margaret has got the income which is net of standard rate tax, the regime is special anyway because the annuity is taxed in part only. The major part of it is seen as a return of capital. The big thing is that you, Frank, want to keep control of the capital, is that right?"

"Yes" he said. "We might need it for another business in years to come. And they could change the milkman!!"

"Well, let us put the whole thing in a box, such that the capital is tied up and returned to you Frank at the end of the ten years, whilst Margaret has the pleasure of the income, during the currency of the policy"

And that was the deal done.

This marvellous contract provides a guaranteed income of £5.202.07 per quarter for Margaret to spend [and we do know that the ladies like to spend] and Frank is secure in the knowledge that at the end of ten years, the Revertor to Settlor Trust will deliver the cash value of the endowment portion of the policy to him in the region of £140,000 tax-free from the £74,631 guaranteed sum assured. Based upon a similar scheme maturing today.

A win win situation.

IMPORTANT NOTE:

If a divorce ensues this type of arrangement would need the consent of **both** parties to surrender. **BE SURE** that the relationship is sound.

Case Study 2

John came out of the Air Force as a fitter. He studied the markets and what he should do with his gratuity and made two very wise decisions.

The first was to become employed by the National Freight Corporation and buy some of their shares. The second was to take out a Back to Back scheme that would supplement his income at a known level, over a ten year period and yet increase the value of his capital to give it some proof against inflation.

He took out the Back to Back in 1979. Inflation had been quite high, interest rates were falling, and the quotations from the company showed maturity values for the underlying with profit policy sum assured of £1,694 [these were pre-LAUTRO days].

The income that John would enjoy, over that ten year period was £449 per annum, paid half yearly.

John's wife was a very cautious woman and took a lot of persuading to allow him to put his hard-earned money into an insurance product, but ten years later it was she who was pressing to repeat the exercise having, of course, taken some of the profit from the original scheme! It had delivered what was promised plus extra.

The original quoted maturity value for that ten year endowment was £1,694 and the actual amount paid to John and his wife at the end of the ten years was £4,515.

ON TOP OF THAT THEY ENJOYED AN INCOME NET OF TAX OVER THE TEN YEAR PERIOD OF £4,490.

The interesting thing with this case is that our task was merely to see if we could provide the same, or a higher, level of income than the income foregone by taking a £3,000 commutation value from John's service pension.

The annuity was provided by Eagle Star and the endowment by Friends Provident.

Mr. Moles Greenhouse

___16___

THE GREENHOUSE EFFECT

How do you describe investment in a single premium whole life policy - an Investment Bond? Why should people invest in a Bond? Surely Unit Trusts would be just as good, more flexible than a Bond. Perhaps even direct investment in shares might be better?

I liken a Bond to a greenhouse. For those of you who are not gardeners, a greenhouse is a glass structure where plants can be reared in controlled conditions. The atmosphere is controllable. Pest and disease control is made easier. Crops can be grown 'out of season'.

To my mind a Bond is a transparent structure where investments can be reared in controlled conditions.

If we plant seedlings or mature plants in the garden, they are exposed to wind, rain, strong sunlight, drought, over watering, pests, predators and disease. Money when it is invested is very similar.

If invested here and there without too much real thought, it gets overgrown by weeds [building societies might bring out new savings contracts which reduces the interest rate on existing contracts - without notification - that sort of weed]. Weeds constrain growth.

In the garden pests; and viruses get at the plant and restrict it's growth by sucking out the sap to serve its own parasitic appetite. The plant needs the sap to grow.

Financial investments are the same. Management charges,

commissions, Income Tax, Capital Gains Tax and other taxes can all reduce the facility and ability of the money to grow.

How then does a Bond help?

I explain to my clients:-

"Our Bond is like a greenhouse in Kew Gardens. In Kew Gardens I think you would agree they have professional gardeners who make sure that the greenhouse conditions are ideal. Just enough moisture, sufficient air humidity, the temperature is right, not too much sunlight.

The diseased crop can be pruned and removed quickly before it has a chance to affect the whole environment. Pesticides, compost, manure can all be applied in the correct proportions to achieve the best possible expectation of results. That is not to say that Kew Gardens greenhouses are free from mishap. The chance of mishap is, however, greatly reduced. The prospect for growth is enhanced tremendously."

Our financial greenhouse, the investment Bond, is no different. Professional Fund Managers oversee a varied crop of property, equity, gilt and specialist area investments to reduce the risk of mishap and enhance the prospect of a good and enhancing harvest.

One of the other things we can do with a greenhouse is grow lettuce all year round. WHAT THE HELL HAS LETTUCE GOT TO DO WITH FINANCIAL PLANNING? Nothing. Except that many of the people that you are talking to understand gardening and do not understand financial planning. Money makes them nervous, worried, apprehensive, concerned. Gardening gives them comfort, pleasure, enjoyment, satisfaction, return and many other things.

By linking in with a client's thought pattern on gardening, I have found that they identify with what we are endeavouring to tell them. Growing lettuces out of doors all year round is impossible in England. Similarly with some investments you cannot regulate the time at which the income will be generated and, therefore, when a tax liability may arise because it is in the contract. A "gilt" dividend is paid twice per year on a set date. Building Societies pay interest on a set date. Even if the interest is reinvested it still arises on that date and it is still subject to tax at that date. Unit Trusts are the same. A BOND IS DIFFERENT.

The Bond is like a greenhouse. We can generate income as and when we want it. In other words the investor controls his crop. He can regulate his harvest and, therefore, he can regulate his tax liability.

That is controlling pests. That is saving waste. That is making the most out of one's resources.

Now because illustrations help folk to understand, you should assist your explanation of the greenhouse principle with drawings because it gives a visual "look" to the concept.

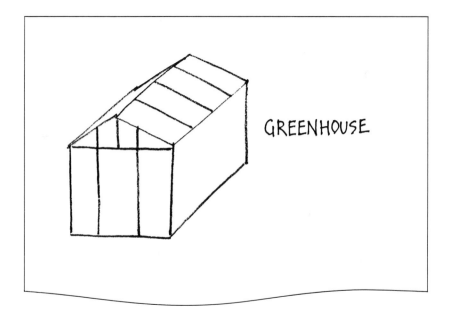

"If you take your £20,000 and put it into the greenhouse, then we straight away protect it from the elements. Do you agree with that?"

"Obviously there is the cost of building the greenhouse and that is the bid to offer spread and just as with the greenhouse it is a one-off cost up front."

"Once your £20,000 is in the greenhouse, we can control where it is invested just the same as growing crops. We can have some tomatoes, some lettuce, some radishes, some peppers, what have you. In the Bond we have property, equities, gilts and so on and **you** can either decide what crops you will grow or you let a manager do that for you in a Managed Fund; a head gardener if you like.

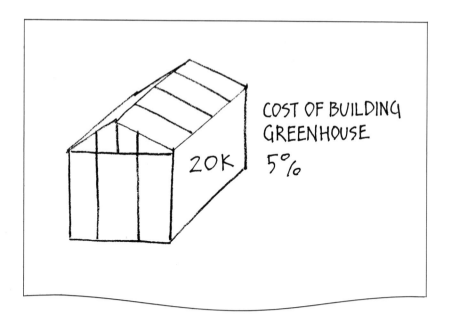

COST OF BUILDING
GREENHOUSE
20K 5%

It is a bit like a commercial greenhouse really, We look to sell our crops for profit at the end of the day, don't we?

The main thing we want is a steady flow of produce from our crops to keep us from going hungry. Within the Bond, what we might want is a monthly income. We can produce that. We might want an ad hoc crop, well we only want tomatoes and lettuce during the summer. Fine, we might only want to withdraw from the Bond on odd occasions. We might not want any withdrawals during some years - we could be growing future seed.

The thing is that within our greenhouse - the Bond - we can keep disease and pests away such as unwelcome tax bills or losses because of market slippage. Equities might be going down, therefore, we can move into property or gilts. Property may become uncertain, therefore, we will move our investment somewhere else within the greenhouse. In other words we will grow different crops. We will prune back. At the end of the day we have one of the most cost effective and tax efficient vehicles that is available for planning your financial resources. They would otherwise be subject to personal Income Tax, Capital Gains Tax or Inheritance Tax.

Marrow Barrow

Case Study 1

The Greenhouse Bond

Barbara Carter, an elderly widow, relies on investment income to supplement her State Pension and a professional teacher's pension to keep body and soul together.

When I first saw Barbara in 1983, her mother was still alive [in her nineties.] Barbara had a hotch potch of investments in shares and building societies, together with a large number of local council bonds, which provided a regular income twice yearly.

Her problem [although she did not recognise it as a problem] was that the tax man was stripping away large chunks of her investment return and her capital was losing value.

Barbara is a gardener. She loves her garden. She has a tit box and hangs up peanuts, cuts up bacon rind, sorts out the sparrows and befriends the robin. She has a man in to tend the garden, but she oversees that tending with a knowledgeable diligence. Barbara might not understand money, but she does understand plants, flowers and vegetables. She knows how a greenhouse works.

In July 1983 we set up a Sun Life Bond from a share exchange with an initial investment of £23,052.66. We explained that by moving some of the crops [the investment money] out of the greenhouse and into cloches or a cold frame, we could actually harden the crops off for when they had to survive on their own [in ten years time].

Mrs Carter set up a maximum investment plan at a gross premium of £750 p.a. which, with the benefit of life insurance premium relief, brought the actual premium down to £637 per annum, which is about where it is today. A recent valuation of the 'crops' showed that they had grown to over £51,000 and in 1993, Barbara will have the benefit of a maturing policy bond within her cold frame [Maximum Investment Plan] to draw tax free income from, for the rest of her life.

This particular arrangement was only part of an overall strategy, but the greenhouse has worked and the "cloches" have all but hardened the crops off for the "real world" in 1993, and beyond, when this arrangement takes over from her current income producing mechanism.

Case Study 2

I shall never forget the case of Peter Baxter.

Peter was the result of a cold call. He ran a hotel and was thirty years older than his wife.

Over the years I worked on doing little bits here and there and generally being around "in the picture." One day the picture changed. Peter had decided that he was going to sell the hotel and I was alerted to the fact that he would need to invest the proceeds of the sale. Over the next eighteen months to two years, Peter's view of how he should invest and what he should invest in ebbed and flowed from a major hotel to a development project to cash on the Stock Market to golf balls in Bahrain [I lied about the golf balls!]

At the end of two years, we had set up a couple of greenhouse schemes, a Bond with Norwich Union and another with Scottish Amicable, based upon the principle of "capital conversion". The "greenhouse" plants are systemically "thinned" out into cloches to harden off for ten years from inception of the scheme to provide tax free income.

But we still had not got the main crop into the greenhouse.

The main crop, as I saw it, was the £200,000 that was planted in wasteland, bugs and aphides in the shape of the tax man attacking one section of the crops, drought and indecision taking their toll of other parts as the Stock Market ebbed and flowed together with cost of moving in or out prohibiting incisive movement.

The one thing that motivated Peter was tax. He really did not like paying tax, and yet here he was resolved to the fact that he would pay it because "he had to."

I sat down at my computer one afternoon and I worked through late into that night and the following night, and probably a few more days and nights after that to devise a program that would show Peter just what was happening to his money. Eventually I had it, I 'phoned Peter up.

"Peter, I talked to you about the greenhouse concept and you know about greenhouses because you have got two, can I come and show you a new insecticide that will stop the bugs eating your money?"

Well he laughed. "You can come over" he said "but it will

probably not do you any good"

I descended on Peter on a day in 1983, about half way through the morning carrying my 'portable' computer. It weighed half a ton and was as big as a bed-side locker.

"I've just brought my spray gun" I said.

He was tickled pink, he thought it was all very, very funny.

I took it into the dining room and set everything up. I had a full analysis on the screen of what he had invested and where;

"Peter", I said, "look at the screen and tell me if that is a true picture of where you are invested at the moment, give or take a few bob?" He confirmed that it was.

"Let's have a look at how much the aphides are eating. How much of your crop is being destroyed?", and we went down to the bottom of this program and there was the tax - £56,670 odd of it.

"That is how much tax you are paying Peter" said I "and here is my special insecticide" and I flicked back up into the program. I took £180,000 from a little block nominated for the building society investments and moved it down into the space for a bond. I allocated 5% tax deferred income for Peter to spend.

I then shifted the cursor on the screen down to the bottom of the program where it said 'TAX TO PAY' and I said

"Right Peter, if we put your money in the greenhouse and stop the vermin getting at it, this is what the saving will be, watch that box" and I pointed to the box where the £56,670 was, because it was still up there - £56,670.

I then pressed the appropriate keys to make the program re-calculate. In a flash the figure changed to £36,490 in front of his eyes. He could not believe it.

"Do I really save that much" he said

"Peter" said I "you save £20,000 a year in tax, that is what I have been trying to tell you for the last two years"

"Well - what are we waiting for" he said "let's get the money in the greenhouse" and that is exactly what we did.

The Pocket Calculator

17

COMPUTER FRIENDLY

Installing a computer can be a trauma that starts at conception, proceeds through the most uncertain of pregnancies and finally, to a large number of hapless individuals, gives birth to a demon of unassailable proportions. Does it have to be so? Good business practice when one is hiring an individual to do a job is to outline the tasks that that particular person will undertake in your organisation and set them down as a job specification.

Employing a computer to do a job is no different. Managing a business in my book is a matter of applying techniques that others have found produce good results. Somebody gave me this very valuable piece of advice.

A job specification is essential in choosing the equipment and the programs.

Lay out the work that you want completed in an orderly fashion on an A4 sheet of paper. Please do not extend your job list to more than one sheet, because you will almost certainly fail to find a solution to your problem. List the specified tasks and no more.

A typical job specification would be:

[1]   **To calculate present and future values of lump sums.**

[2]   **To calculate mortgage repayments at any level of interest over any given term.**

[3] To calculate the amount outstanding on a loan at any point during the term of the loan.

[4] Must fit in inside jacket pocket.

[5] No print out required.

[6] No internal light required

That was the job specification for the Sharp PC 1211 which I had to program and use daily.

The programming requirement was optional and, therefore, I did not include it on my original job specification to be programmed for me or for me to do the job. The computer has many other functions but that is irrelevant at the "job specification" juncture.

The Trade Fair Technique

Having decided what we want the computer program to achieve, the next task is to find software that will actually produce it. It is disarming to consider how many individuals buy hardware to solve a "computer" problem. A good looking plastic box needs to have efficient software to run in it, therefore, the program is what you must home in on. The Trade Fair Technique is quite simple.

Eighteen years ago, when I was seeking to employ my first computer, I was given advice to use a "job specification" I implemented it at the Cunard Hotel in London. At that time there were eighty trade stands from different manufacturers and software houses exhibiting their wares. Consider the time it would take to have an in depth conversation with each of those program providers. My time span with some was measured in seconds.

With my job specification, neatly written out, with tick boxes next to each particular heading and a space at the top for the name of the provider, I was quickly able to hold my pen against the list, speaking to the accomplished salesman and run down each point on a yes/no basis.

NO BUTS. NO MAYBE. This simple expediency brought my shopping list down from eighty exhibitors to two who could actually fulfil my requirements. By this simple method I had made available to myself over three hours for negotiation and came away from the Trade Fair with what I still consider was the best deal, a bargain price and a firm delivery date. I was, however, to learn two valuable lessons, but more of that later.

The Demonstration Sale

I wonder how many of us I wonder have seen the 'demonstration technique' working wonders with colourful graphs or producing reams of tables and reports all of which look exactly right for us or our clients. The system produces instant analysis of a market, complete amalgamation of the data base with the letters that we are sending out, pre-selection of individual clients by birth date or occupation, just as we and our staff require.

When the computer arrives, it is empty. The demonstration disks, so carefully prepared for our education, probably incorporate facets of the program that have not been finally developed yet - Oh, but they are coming, and soon!

A lot of demonstrations are nothing short of a sham. A technique that I have developed over the umpteen years that I have had computers in my brokerage is - ALWAYS use **your own data.** When the demonstration is over ensure that you have some of **your own material** available to test the system. Sit the operative down who is giving you 'the big deal', and say "fine - just put this data back into your machine, on your program and let's see how it works in practice." On occasions you will see a lot of back pedalling.

Ideally what you should do is complete all of the tasks with your own data as listed on your original job sheet. No excuses: that is key.

No matter how pretty it looks, make sure that the job can be done with the program and hardwork that you are going to buy.

That also applies when buying peripherals. If you are buying a printer or an electronic typewriter to work with your system, make sure that the supplier fits it and shows it working **before** you pay for it.

We had the situation where for two years an 'Imperial 5005' electronic typewriter had been working with our "Apricot" computer using "Wordstar" software. We needed another printer. Our local supplier had an 'Imperial 5015'. We were assured that it would work, but we insisted on going back to basic principles. The supplier's technician was in and out of our office for three weeks before they finally gave up and agreed that some peculiarity in the electronics of the '5015' would not allow it to do what the '5005' would do. Yet the two machines looked pretty well identical.

Giving Birth.

The delivery of the hardware and its associated wizardry to your home or office will be a big day. You will never, ever, forget it. Every computer system that I have ever seen installed has been wished to hell and back more times than enough during its first three to six months of "life". Soothing the beast with raw data, and the resultant frequent bilious attacks that spew paper and foul language far and wide can test the best of temperaments. The instructions say one thing and the machine demands another. Communication skills are non existent in the computer industry. Computerese and gobbledegook are related languages. Telephone lines glow red hot and many a nervous breakdown is precipitated by an uncontrolled head long dive into the do-it-yourself learning routine. Don't do it.

[1]   **E nsure before your machine is delivered that a competent engineer will accompany it and not leave your premises until it is working. Make sure that this fact is written down.**

[2]   **E nsure that once the installation engineer has left with everything working smoothly, a training administrator comes to give you adequate instruction. The alternative if training is not available [you may well have purchased off the shelf packages such as a spreadsheet, a word processing program or a data base program] 'phone round your local area. Information Technology [ITEC - units] and similar will train you, or your staff, at very reasonable rates and avoid an awful lot of the frustration. The thing to ensure is that they are using the same equipment that you are using and not training you to use the software on a different hardware system.**

What makes it all happen?

I have found that the most precious commodity to computer suppliers is good old pounds/pence. They will do almost anything for money! It has been my experience that a retention of at least 10% until all training is complete and the machine is installed and producing what they say it should produce, is a very worthwhile stick with which to beat people when things go wrong.

I said that I had learned two valuable lessons from my first computer purchase. My Olivetti S24 - which incidentally was a superb machine for its day, arrived as a complete assembly. My office at that time was a twenty-eight foot caravan. Caravans have very narrow doors. We had to dismantle the machine to get it in. Having re-assembled it, the technical operator came next day and we spent several days learning how to work the machine. Everything seemed fine.

A peculiarity of caravans is that they suffer from condensation and within a short time my machine was not working at all well. It had a metal case and all sorts of sparks were flying out of the back of it. The first engineer to come and tackle my computer's problems informed me that he would "never have sold me it in the first place." My cash retention bought me a new engineer by switching servicing from Derby to Sheffield. The second engineer was more amenable and after a quick spray with WD40 the machine was never any problem ever again.

Time has moved on but the principles of purchasing a computer system have not changed one jot. The method works. We have adopted it for every one of our ten plus computer systems, all dedicated to different tasks or replacing old out-moded systems like the S24.

Always have a "job specification". Make your choices from the widest possible selection, probably at exhibitions. Make your deal and get everything in writing. Secure some form of retention, installation checks, training and warrenty maintenance. Always use your own data for a demonstration with a "live" program.

Maintenance

This can be a very expensive item. Most contracts seem to allow for RPI increases on an ad hoc basis. If you can avoid maintenance then do so. For most computers that are going into a small business environment, maintenance agreements are irrelevant. Software maintenance is a different matter. Software upgrading is essential.

Maintenance of the hardware; printers, central computers, computer processing units [C.P.Us] etc. all have a warranty and from my experience will go wrong during the first six to twelve months, or they will perform the function that they are purchased for, unless they are abused, for years on end. A good local engineer will usually be available at a fraction of the cost, and will prove to be a cheaper option than an ever increasing maintenance bill that on many occasions buys an inferior service and an inadequate time response.

By preparing yourself, using the method that I have outlined, you need never fear this extremely friendly employee who seldom has a day off, never gets upset, cannot answer back and if treated with respect, will give you years and years of valuable service as a cost efficient workmate.

Partners Policy

18

PARTNERSHIP INSURANCE

"Hello Gordon, thank you for your time, I believe that you are concerned about partnership insurance, how can I help you?"

"Well, it is like this, I am the junior partner in a partnership of four people, and I am a little concerned if anything happened to AB, how would it affect me? I really cannot find the resources to buy out his share of the capital in the firm, and I know that the other senior partner is determined not only to retain his percentage but also to increase it"

"What is the current value of the partnership?"

"I suppose we are looking at about £280,000 net of all the borrowings. I have had to borrow to put my £30,000 in and I tell you it would be a real struggle to sort out the right percentage I would need to buy AB, the senior partner's, share. Well, technically, there are two senior partners by profit share because the partnership is split as follows:

	% of Shares	Approximate Value
AB	35%	100K
CD	35%	100K
EF	18%	50K
GH	12%	30K

"The other worry I have got is that the senior partners have already got life insurance cover, it is EF and myself that are out on a limb, and I don't think they are terribly interested in taking out any more"

"Well, there is no need for them to take out any more if they have sufficient cover to look after their particular patch. Why don't you just insure them for your own benefit?"

"How would we do that?"

"Well, let's have a look at the situation!"

This is when I produce my A4 sheet of paper.

"Because what we are looking at is our four partners."

and I draw the four people concerned

"we have 100K 100K 50K and 30K which equals 280K" Use round figures for convenience.

"Now the thing is, if the first man was to die, then we would be left with 100K 50K and 30K but how would we split up that 100K that currently belongs to AB?"

This is Gordon's dilemma, how much does he insure the senior partner for, because he knows that CD wants precisely the same proportion of benefit if anything happens to his colleague as he has got now.

All Gordon wants to do is make sure he doesn't lose any percentage share that he would get.

"Well, what we have is 150K and your 30K, Gordon, 180K and what we are going to do is use that as our denominator for a series of very small division sums"

"To calculate your own proportion as a percentage of what is left, which is the important thing because that is now the structure of the partnership, we take 30 divided by 180 which gives the result 16.67%" [.1667 x 100]

N.B.: Remember if you have a calculator that has do a constant function, the calculations are simplified.

Put 180 divide divide and then it is just a matter of putting 30 and = . That gives the answer 16.67% [.167 actually which we need to mentally multiply by 100.]

Enter 50 and press = and that shows 27.78, [.2778 just move the decimal place two points to the right.]

Then we want 100 divided by 180 therefore we execute 100, = which produces 55.55

We have 55.55, which we add to the 27.78 together with 16.67. We should get 100; which we do.

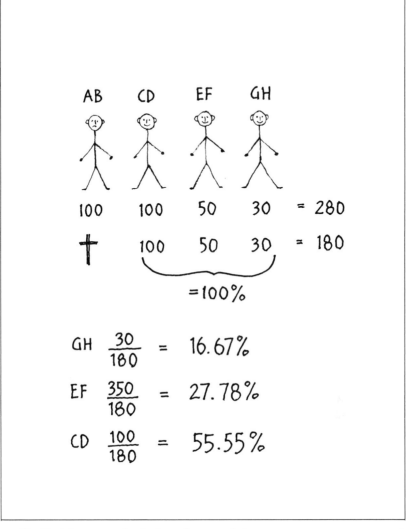

AB   CD   EF   GH

100   100   50   30   = 280

† 100   50   30   = 180

= 100%

GH $\dfrac{30}{180}$ = 16.67%

EF $\dfrac{350}{180}$ = 27.78%

CD $\dfrac{100}{180}$ = 55.55%

So that is our calculation done, of the percentage now owned of the remaining partnership having lost AB [because he has died.]

We can now do the sums that we require by going back to the original partnership to see how much capital we actually need to generate to pay off that £100,000 that AB currently owns.

"In this instance we don't need a calculator because all we have to do is multiply our factor by the amount of the partners' cover: That is 16.67 x 100 that we need to insure AB for, £16,670 for you Gordon"

"EF needs to raise £27,780 and CD needs to raise £55,550 which will give us £100,000 total sum assured."

That has worked out how much life insurance we need on AB.

We can work through and do CD who coincidentally needs the same; then we can do the same for EF.

If you want to run through the exercise again, then I have done that on the calculator. Again a simple calculation just so that you can run through it.

Put the four bodies in, indicate the one that you want to die, that shows you which ones are left and you can then work out your new figures to calculate the percentage of the "new" partnership that exists and that will tell you how you break down the insurance for EF.

In this instance we have AB 100K, CD 100K, EF died, and his partnership share is about 50K. We have got GH at 30K which when added up amounts to 280K. If EF dies then we have 100 plus 100 plus 30 which equals 230K.

£230K becomes our denominator. Plug that into our calculator; 230 divide, divide put in our numerator which in this instance is for GH and is 30K, so put in 30, = , and the answer given is 13.04%. For CD and AB the input will be 100. Put in 100 = and the answer is 43.48. Add a second 43.48 and you can see that that adds up to 100.

That shows the precise sum assured that one needs to have.

You could probably round those up to give them some substance but that at least gives you a reasonably accurate amount of insurance that needs to be taken out on the life of EF by the other three partners to make up the amount of capital that you would need to buy into the partnership share in the same proportion as you had in the original partnership.

We need to do one more simple set of calculations and again I think the match-stick men allow the client to see precisely what is happening and it also ensures that you don't make a mistake. You know which one has died.

Of course, at [c] GH has died therefore we are looking at the insurance that the others will need to take out to pay off his share.

In fact the two senior partners are not bothered about taking the insurance out, therefore, we really need only to work out EFs but we will do them all just to work through it.

The remaining share after GHs death is 250K that becomes our denominator.

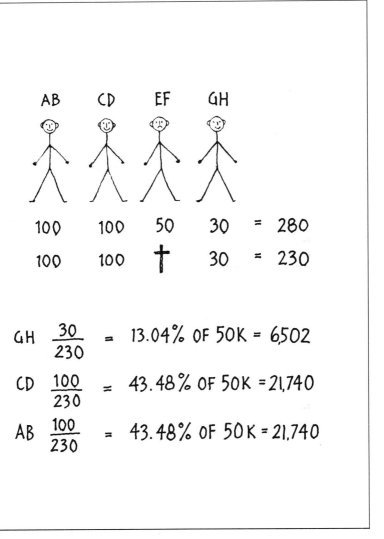

AB   CD   EF   GH

100   100   50   30   =   280

100   100   †   30   =   230

GH $\dfrac{30}{230}$ = 13.04% OF 50K = 6,502

CD $\dfrac{100}{230}$ = 43.48% OF 50K = 21,740

AB $\dfrac{100}{230}$ = 43.48% OF 50K = 21,740

EF has 50 of that so that goes on the top. Again using our constant put in the following sequence. 250; divide; divide; 50; =. The answer is .2 which is 20%. [Move the decimal place two points to the right].

CD will need 100 over 250 and AB will need the same. We do not need a calculator for this, but we can do it if we need it. .4 is the answer, which is 40%. We can then work on to the next item which is to say that EF would be entitled to 20% of £30,000 [GHs share] which is £6,000. The other two would have £12,000 each.

AB   CD   EF   GH

100   100   50   30   = 280

100   100   50   †   = 250

$$EF \quad \frac{50}{250} = 20\% \text{ OF } 30\text{K} = 6{,}000$$

$$CD \quad \frac{100}{250} = 40\% \text{ OF } 30\text{K} = 12{,}000$$

$$AB \quad \frac{100}{250} = 40\% \text{ OF } 30\text{K} = 12{,}000$$

"Now Gordon; having established how much insurance you need to take out on the others: you can see from this matrix, what you need should AB die. ABs share as far as you are concerned would demand £16,900 of cover on his life. You would need to complete £16,900 on CD and to secure your percentage of EFs partnership share you would need £6,502. Given the premiums that I have here, the cost will be £42.03 per month - less than £10 per week to look after your capital interests in the firm.

From EFs point of view, he will have to find about £15.55 per week to pay for your capital share and we really only have to establish whether that is acceptable to you. We have established that the two major share partners do not wish to take any further action. All we need to do is to complete proposal forms on their lives. The policies will be written under Trust (because of minimum premiums if we did them all life of another).

We will prepare them all as separate policies, under Trust, with the appropriate proportion for the moment between EF and GH written into the Trust''.

The thing is,by doing the partnership insurance this way, the partner can see precisely how you calculated the sums assured and in my experience they are more inclined, more assured that they are doing the right thing, in the right amounts to solve their problem. Although it is academic it is usual for you to be dealing with academic people. These individuals are linear thinkers, therefore, they want to see the figures and they want to have proof positive that that is what is going on.

The fact that you then scale up and do £30,000 instead of £27,000 or £20,000 instead of £16,900 is irrelevant. What you have done is proved the theory and this method allows you to do that.

The other thing it allows you to do is to show in matrix form the precise cost. You can show that in weekly amounts or monthly. Here the accounts would probably be done on a monthly basis because the premiums will be taken from the partnership account monthly.

A further thing the matrix does is that it allows you to produce more than one possible outcome. A matrix can be produced showing just death in service.

You can do as I have done on the illustration. Show death in service plus critical illness. In the event of death or critical illness the partnership share value is available in cash to buy that partner out.

In this case, AB is a lot older than the other three partners and, therefore, is going to retire much earlier. You could actually show death in service and critical illness if you wanted to, however an endowment return at aged 65 would allow the other partners to buy AB out, use three sets of figures. Present those to allow the partners to choose how they they want to satisfy their circumstances. In this instance they chose the middle ground and took out the death in service plus critical illness.

"Fourteen column" analysis sheets are useful to have in the office for presentations of this nature.

DEATH IN SERVICE PLUS CRITICAL ILLNESS

	AB		CD		LF		GH	
% ORIGINAL PARTNERSHIP	35% 100K		35% 100K		18% 50K		12% 30K	
PARTNER BUYING INS.					SA	COST	SA	COST
AB	——		55,550	100.39	27,780	50.23	16,670	30.76
CD	55,550	28.18			27,780	14.13	16,670	8.65
EF	21,740	8.74	21,740	8.74			6,502	2.62
GH	12,000	6=	12,000	6=	6,000	3=		
TOTAL FROM PARTNERS ACCT.	42.95		115.13		67.36		42.03	

Case Study 1

Partnership Insurance

Today L.T.D is a thriving partnership and in common with the majority of firms it has a very interesting history of expansion and growth, contraction and re-trenching, partner retirement and "buy out" together with death and disability.

I first started working with L.T.D. in the early seventies. John Smith and Paul Jones were the senior partners Graham Green, Mark Andrews and Bob Turner were all around thirty years of age, some fifteen years junior to the senior partners and there was some younger blood coming through.

My initial task in 1977 was to set up partnership insurances to ensure that the capital value of the firm was protected and a deceased partner's share could be bought out.

I stated that there had been a death, but what I did not say was that it was quite recent. It was one of those three erstwhile thirty year olds who, at the time of his death was in his mid-forties.

I will concentrate on Mark Andrew's insurances because by widening the view and ignoring all the boring detail you, the reader, will have a clearer understanding of how the system actually works [or in this case worked].

In 1977 we set up policies for Mark in the sum of £24,244 through a whole life non-profit policy [guaranteed return] at a premium of £19.10 per month under a Partnership Trust. He was one of five. By 1980, John Smith had retired from the partnership due to severe ill health. We had received a surrender value for his whole life policy, apportioned that as a cash value against his share of the profits and transferred the whole life policy out of Trust for the partners and into a Trust for his wife and family. John had a major health problem and could not have purchased life assurance on the open market. Level term insurance would have been useless in his circumstances.

In the meantime two new partners had joined the firm; Adrian Curtis and Alfred Jinks. New policies were set up for them and increases were also arranged for the other four partners. In Mark's case a new policy was set up for a sum assured of £7,756 at an additional premium of £7.39 per month. Again, on a guaranteed benefit whole life policy with Norwich Union written under Trust.

In 1984 a further review was carried out when a new partner Barry Stoneham joined the firm. There were six offices to operate, compared to the original four. Things were going well, property values had risen sharply and we now had to put in further insurance which in Mark's case meant another £26,000 whole life guaranteed payment policy at a premium of £26.36 per month.

Once again, all of the Trust Deeds had to be altered and the policies juggled about to accommodate the new names. Our client firm was on growing.

In 1989 the policies had to be adjusted yet again. Major purchases of five new office premises occurred and, in May, two new partners Donald and James were brought in. A further policy for £22,000, at a premium of £22.23 per month, was added to Mark's portfolio, but this time with a low cost whole life policy. Norwich Union had ceased to underwrite whole life non-profit assurance because there was little demand for it. [we were still requesting it but apparently no one else in the market place was].

Guaranteed benefit policies were seen as poor value for money by many pundits.

In mid 1990/early 1991 the housing recession was well underway, overheads of the firm had soared to an all time high, putting pressure on borrowing and every other aspect of trading. All but one of the new offices that had been purchased just a couple of years earlier had to be sold and the partnership re-arranged yet again.

One of the existing partners bought the five offices and moved out and again the Trusts were altered and the policy maintained in full force to move with Donald to his new "company." After all, whole life insurance is designed to last for a lifetime. The surrender value was once again calculated and its value off-set against the amount required for settlement following the change of partner.

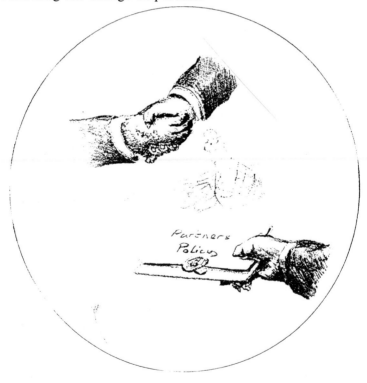

Tragically in September, 1991 Mark died and it is a tribute to the life insurance industry that just the existence of those four policies persuaded the bank to re-open the partnership trading account which they had closed immediately on hearing the news of Mark's death.

The bank maintained full overdraft facilities in the certain knowledge that the partners were financially sound through these policies and the Key-man policy which reduced their exposure. Most important of all, the partners did not have to worry. There was no need to be concerned because they knew benefits were on hand.

Policies that were set up for all of the partners had continuation option clauses. That particular clause in these policies allowed extra insurance to be taken out free of underwriting on pre-determined anniversaries.

Paul Jones, the second of the senior partners that I mentioned as being part of the firm in 1977, had developed one or two health impediments that would have certainly created underwriting problems resulting in increased premium payments had it not been for the options available to him. Needless to say he exercised every one of them as well as taking out some other "loaded" insurances which were essential for his family's needs. His son needed constant care following an accident.

The options were also a regular reminder that the cover needed reviewing for all the partners. The premiums were treated as drawings and apportioned as shown in the main chapter.

Of the ten 'personalities' involved in our financial planning for this firm since 1977, two have developed life threatening conditions and one has died [from the middle age grouping.].

Abacus Mole

___ 19 ___

LARGE PREMIUMS

Very often when we are talking about partnership insurance, key man insurance, the premiums can be quite substantial and I can best illustrate how I deal with the situation by discussing basically what happens at a meeting with the directors of a substantial construction company.

Hugh the Managing Director was quite concerned about the level of premium and I felt that he was getting a different perspective on the situation than he had originally had. He appreciated the problems that would be caused within the company, particularly on his death, the bank would probably foreclose, or at least freeze the account, the rest of the board members and, of course, close family would suffer as a result.

"Hugh" I said "What is your turnover?"

"Our turnover?"

and I pulled out my pocket calculator, one of those about the size of a credit card, and whilst he was thinking I punched in the premium that we had been discussing, which was £2,760 p.a.

"err around £2.3 million I think" he said after some time.

"£2.3 million" I repeated, pressed the divide key and said "well let us divide the premium by that £2.3 million"

"2300000" I then offered the calculator towards him, "is that right?"

"yep" he said with a puzzled look on his face, and then I pressed the equals sign .0012.

"Tell me something Hugh, is that a big number or a little number?"

his face broke into a smile, and he could see how insignificant in business terms, in turnover terms, the premium was.

The problem initially was that he had been looking at the situation in personal terms. The key to his perception and understanding was to actually place the premium in turnover terms so that he thought about it on the balance sheet or the profit and loss account and not in his own personal account.

"O.K." he said with a chuckle "let's complete the papers"

Please don't thank me for this idea it came from Roger Zena at one of the Life Insurance Association's Barbican conventions, which just goes to prove how valuable the Conventions are. You should never miss one.

Stuffing the Cow!

═ 20 ═

MONEY DOWN
THE DRAIN

Ask any media mogel or consumerist and they will tell you.
"Paying Taxes? - it's money down the drain"
We, and our clients, see a heafty percentage of our taxes as being
paid in vain. What do we get in return for all the taxes??

Yes - it's just money down the drain, and Inheritance Tax more
than most.

You work all your life paying taxes on everything you earn. There
is tax to pay on investments which go up by a bob or two and they
(the revenue) still want their pound of flesh when you are dead and
buried. It's money down the drain.

I occasionally find myself in deep discussion with clients over
the amount of tax that will be payable on their death. Inheritance
Tax can be paid by instalments, therefore, they point out that the
children will have a farm or an office block or whatever the asset
happens to be that will produce income and that will enable the
next generation to pay whatever is due to the Government.

That is all well and good, I point out, but what if the asset does
not produce enough to pay the tax, then surely they are going to
have to borrow. In any event, they can only pay the tax out of net
income, after they have paid tax on what they have earned, or on
capital growth from an asset that they eventually sell.

Well - they can borrow can't they? Surely if there is any shortfall they can borrow against the asset and pay the tax that way?

"When I am gone, it's their problem"

or

"I started with nothing, why shouldn't they?"

"Let me just ask you the question; did you build all this up just to give it away?"

"No. Of course I didn't build it up just to give it away, but I don't see why we should use the money that we've got now to fund for something that might not happen for another twenty years. I don't want to give any of it away now because I might need it. I use everything as security for borrowing so that I can in fact build the business up or buy more property ...." or whatever their current aspiration or project happens to be.

"Tell me somthing, do you think life insurance is a good investment or a bad investment?"

and the usual response that I get is

"What do you mean?"

I say "well if we were putting £160 per month away to create a quarter of a million pounds worth of life insurance on the death of yourself and your wife, but only payable when you are dead of course, would that be a good investment or a bad investment?"

Given the explanation, the individual usually replies;

"It is a bad investment"

The snappy come back has to be:

"I agree with you, as an investment, life insurance must be one of the poorest investments, one of the worst investments, that you could possible have, wouldn't you agree?"

"Yes"

They are now sensing that there is a catch but perhaps not being astute enough to recognise where the catch is coming from.

"Can I ask you another question?"

"Certainly"

"What's this?"

(drawing left hand side of my A4 sheet - a "matchstick" cow)

"A cow, they say"

"That's good," I reply

"What's this?"

(another drawing on the right hand side of a bucket)

"A bucket?"

"Yes, that's good"

"What do we get in the bucket from the cow?"

By this time, they are getting very quizical

"Milk I suppose"

"Correct" [a line across the bucket is drawn and a label below it confirms 'milk'

"Now let me ask you another question. Your buildings, farm, shares (whatever assets we've been talking about), are they cow or milk?"

Most people reply cow immediately because they recognise that an asset produces something else, the asset in itself is comparable to the cow.

"Terrific."

"What does that produce?"

"Income"

"Is income cow or milk?"

"Milk"

"Good"

"Now what's this?"

(another drawing bottom left)

"I don't know,"they say

"Let me ask you another question, is Inheritance Tax money put to good use for you?"

"No," and they usually laugh, "you've got to be joking."

"It's money down the drain', " right?"

"Yes - it certainly doesn't do any good for me"

"So, if it's money down the drain, what do you think that is?"

"A drain"

"Correct"

"I think you would agree that the taxman's money, "Inheritance Tax" is money down the drain. So lets assume that you've just gone to heaven. You died yesterday. Your beneficiaries, the children, are sat around a table in the kitchen, saying

"What are we going to do about this Inheritance Tax"

and you're sat up there, with your wife, looking down and St Peter comes along in his pink Landrover Discovery and says,

"You got a problem?"

"Yes, the kids are in a bit of difficulty down there but we don't seem to be able to do anything."

He says

"I tell you what, you can both go down there and help them sort it out."

Snaps his fingers: here you are in the kitchen with the kids.

They say

"Well we have the Inheritance Tax to pay, we can either pay it out of income over a period of time or out of capital over a period of time, or we can pay it straight away but we really don't know

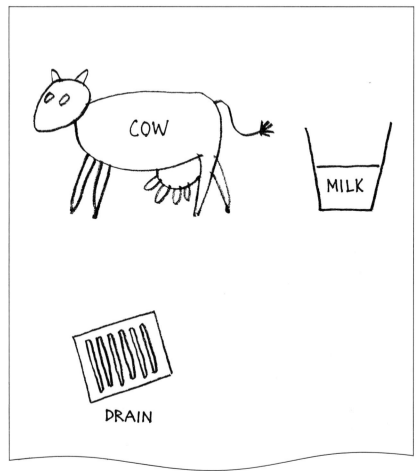

what to do.''

Now what are you going to tell them? Sell the farm, try and pay it out of income, or if they've got some investments, sell them.

They've got a couple of crummy whole life insurances, some shares, a whole stack of gilt edge stock and various other investments, the buildings, the farm etc. Now let me just ask you another question.''

"If they have to put one of the investments down the Government's drain, would you tell them to put your best investments or your worst investment down the drain.''

Is he going to say the best investments? Not usually.

"Well the worst investments of course''

"What's the worst possible investment that you can think of out of this list?''

"The life assurance, property, shares, car, Government Stock, Business Assets", which of those is the poorest, the worst investment? What did you tell me was the worst investment just a few moments ago?"

"The life assurance"

"Given the choice would you advise the children to put cow or milk down the Government's drain?"

"Milk"

"Why?"

"Because the cow will always produce more milk, so you put milk down and milk is income, right?"

The person replies "that is right"

"So if we could take some of the milk from your cow, your investments at the moment, and put it into life assurance do you think that would solve the childrens problems and you could get back to enjoying yourself in heaven?",

AND THEN BE QUIET.

Now I have to thank Roger Zena, an American Million Dollar Round Table Member for that idea which I modified to good old fashioned anglo saxon.

Nothing's new, but I think you'll agree that the perspective of the client has changed and he begins to see the value of life assurance. By taking milk as the herd increases, more milk is produced and a very small proportion of that milk, if it's put to one side in a very poor investment, can actually keep the whole of the estate intact (the herd, if you will) for the next generation to build on even further.

Simplicity doesn't end there because, of course, the next thing to decide is how much to insure for. Again, Roger Zena provided terminology which I have used and failed to better.

"Now what we have to decide is, how much we need to put into life assurance to protect your family. Is that right?"

"Yes"

We have two methods of working. The first is a fee paying method where we produce a twelve page questionnaire to establish all the various facets of your estate and we get the accountants and the lawyers and go over the figures to establish to the penny what your liability will probably be and then we round it up and we say you should buy "a bloc."

"What's a bloc?"
It's £500,000 of whole life assurance.
"Oh"
Or there's method B which is;

"we take a look at your estate and think what it might be like over the next ten years and decide that over the next ten years you'll probably need.....about "a bloc" of life assurance.

Which method would you like to adopt?"

People like choice and of course it's not as simple as we make it out to be. We need to do the job properly, of course. What the client needs to know is that he can trust our judgement. It is also imperative that he understands what we are doing and why. This A4 presentation meets that requirement.

Case Study

I found this quite an amusing case study. I was talking to two twin brothers and their wives about Inheritance Tax and they were having difficulty in getting the perception of the problem into focus. Yes they had got assets, but could not the children just sell the assets or take ten years to pay the tax, why plan ahead and why take out life insurance.

So it came down to the test

"Do you think that like insurance is a bad investment?"

"Well, yes, there is nothing in it for us"

"It is all dead money, it is for the next generation"

"So you think it is probably one of the worst investments that you could probably make?"

"Well - yes, that's right"

"Well let me show you something then" I said
and I got my A4 pad and I drew my picture.

"What is that?" I said

"A cow"

"Correct, and if that is a cow, what is this?"
and I went through the presentation.

Then I said "what sort of yield does your cow have, what assets in cash terms, what percentage?"

They thought for a bit and they said

"Well - about 6%"

and I said "what we are looking for is about 1%, which would leave you with 5%"

"That's right" they said.

"That would leave the cow, or should I say the herd, to grow and be passed on intact to your three daughters and one son" and they bought the concept.

I said that this was an amusing case study; and that is because the two brothers ran a dairy farm and their comments at the end of my presentation were

"Are you setting us up, did you set this up especially for us?"

They were suitably impressed.

21

GLOOMY ROOMS
AND QUILL PENS

The greatest way to improve your client service is to have a good backroom system operating. It never ceases to amaze me how sales people complain about administration and do nothing about it.

The requirement is for YOU to take responsibility for your own actions.

Do you expect other people to put their hand in their pocket to help you achieve what you need to achieve? They will do in the end; because they will have to once they have seen the way you work.

Work smarter, not harder. Employ people who are good at typing, answering the telephone, making appointments, sorting out illustrations, whatever task you need doing and then get on with your primary task using as much of your time as you possible can effectively.

I have a two-thirds/one-third rule. If you are spending more than one third of your time on tasks that are not allied to your main expertise, [or from another standpoint if you have up to two-thirds of your time spent doing administration or other ancillary tasks], then you are on your way out of business, employ good quality assistance.

Administration demands expenditure of time, effort and money. Administration does not directly produce income. Having said that, there are facets of it that are income producing - like devising one page A4 presentations for a particular insurance or investment scheme.

Make the majority of sales appointments yourself.

I know that there are some people who are extremely successful at using a tele-sales technique through hired staff. However, the majority of us probably work with the type of people who like to deal with us personally and are working from referrals and recommendations.

The initial sales contact, therefore, should come from a sales person. You, the sales professional.

All of the follow up work should come from your staff. Chasing medicals, completing the files and discussing matters with the insurance company, so that you know precisely where any case is at any one time.

In my own practice we use a Progress Sheet. Some of my colleagues use a progress board and move cards across the board as the underwriting progresses through the various stages. Take time to devise a system that works for you. Go and see what other people, who are successful in your eyes, are doing. It may be a transferable idea that you can pick up on. The main thing is, HAVE A SYSTEM.

SET UP SYSTEMS

Time management is a high priority subject all on its own, it is important to know where you are, what you are supposed to be doing whilst keeping track of time and costs.

The first question that I ask anybody who comes into my office for advice is "How can I help you"?

"Good morning, my name is Terry O'Halloran, how can I help you?"

Even if they have outlined their problem on the telephone to my staff, who are making the appointment to come into my office, I still ask the question, "how can I help you"? It means that I am in control of the conversation. I have expressed a wish to be of service and that is so important to the person who has come to see me.

To me it does not really matter whether you are employed or self-employed, a company man or an independent. The main thing that matters is that your records are sufficiently detailed to be of use to you;...now, and in the future.

Always use a dictaphone for notes and letters. Dictation transcribers and simple word processors cost little and earn lots.

Dictating a letter, once you get used to it, halves letter writing time at least. An audio typist can fair fly through a tape whereas longhand notes are usually a problem with additions etc. You can speak several times faster than you can write which allows you more time solving other people's problems.

Hod Mole

22

Yo-Yo
PENSION
PLANNING

The principle of carrying back and carrying forward has always presented difficulties for the professional pensions adviser to understand, and it becomes even more difficult to explain verbally to the average client.

When confronted with this particular topic we have to remember certain key facts. We can only carry-back into the previous year, unless there are special provisions regarding losses, which allow us to go back further. An employee can only go back one year, in any event.

Carry-back is only available if there is no occupational pension scheme in the year concerned, or a complete refund from an occupational scheme has been granted. This would be the position if, say, the person had been in an occupational scheme less than two years and was under twenty-six years of age. In these circumstances, the individual could elect to have all their contributions repaid and the occupational pension scheme effectively treated as if it had never existed.

One should always look at the personal pension capabilities of a client first before advising on a company sponsored occupational pension scheme. Once the occupational pension scheme is in force, that changes the situation for the individual as far as personal pensions are concerned. Remember, an individual cannot contribute to a personal pension and an occupational pension scheme at the same time. It must be one or the other if he only has one source of income.

The carry-back provisions really need to be looked at first. I invariably start with a line with THIS YEAR about two-thirds of the way along it to the righthand end. Drawn about a third of the way down the page. The initial position is that we have to use up, where possible, all of last year's contribution capacity to bring us up to date.

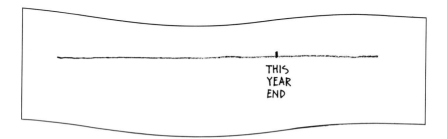

Let us look at last year and see whether you paid any tax during that year. If we take off your personal allowances and look at the net relevant earnings that will indicate the level of taxable income that you actually had. The net relevant earnings, minus personal allowances give us approximately the amount of pension contribution that will maximise the tax rebate for that year.

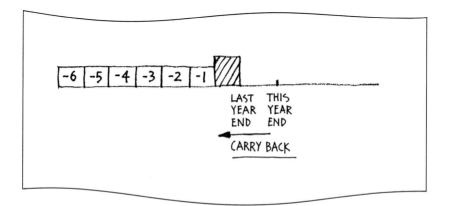

Remember: If you arrange for pension contributions that encroach on your clients' personal tax allowance, you will be losing tax relief because it cannot be taken for both the personal allowance and the pension.

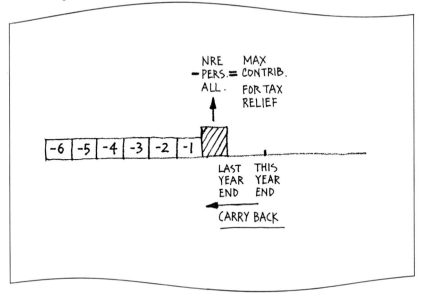

I have drawn a box on the line graph on my A4 sheet of paper and I have written above that N.R.E. × MINUS PERSONAL ALLOWANCE = PERSONAL CONTRIBUTION FOR

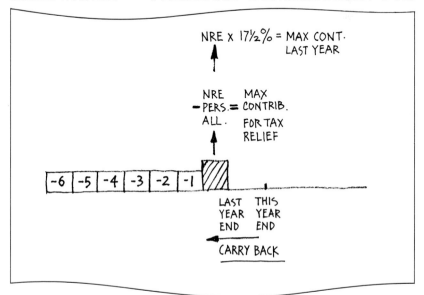

TAX RELIEF. Now we all know that dependent upon the age of the person, so depends the percentage of net relevant earnings that we are actually able to put into pension.

Let us assume this is 17.5%; I write N.R.E. x 17.5% = MAXIMUM CONTRIBUTION FROM LAST YEAR.

Now if we know the numbers, we can put the numbers in. So if your earnings are £20,000 minus the personal allowance of say £5,000 = £15,000 contribution for tax relief and above that £20,000 x 17.5% = £3,500 that he can actually contribute from last year's earnings.

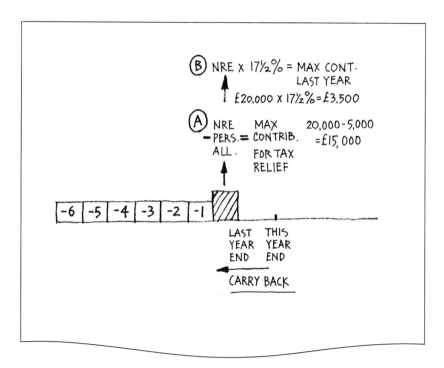

The question is, [I write this half way down the page] HOW DO WE MAKE UP THE DIFFERENCE? and I now letter the maximum contributions for tax relief [a] and the maximum contributions in respect of last year's net relevant earnings [b]. So, therefore [a] minus [b] = 15 K minus 3.5 K = 11.5K and then in brackets [£11.500] There are still a lot of people who do not like the expression "K". It is jargon, if you explain to them that it is shorthand but write it down in longhand when it matters, then they will appreciate that greatly. [Yuppies excepted!]

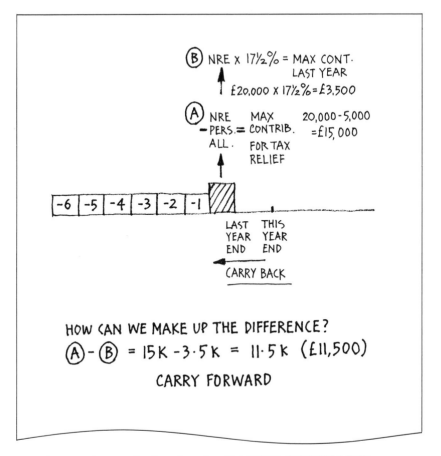

Then underneath that I write CARRY-FORWARD

"What we are actually going to do is carry-forward your earnings, Mr Client, from six years ago. If we can find out your net relevant earnings for the past seven years, we can CARRY BACK into last year and then we can CARRY FORWARD seven years ago up to date, to establish what contributions you were eligible to make to pension in those years but you elected not to make."

"Unfortunately, we cannot use the tax from those years, but we can reclaim some of last year's tax. Let's have a look at how it is done."

Hopefully I will have already been in touch with the accountants, for a self employed person, to get NET RELEVANT EARNINGS for the previous years, or I may know them from their records or the client may have some idea of what they were. Verification from

* Footnote N.R.E.: Net Relevant Earnings

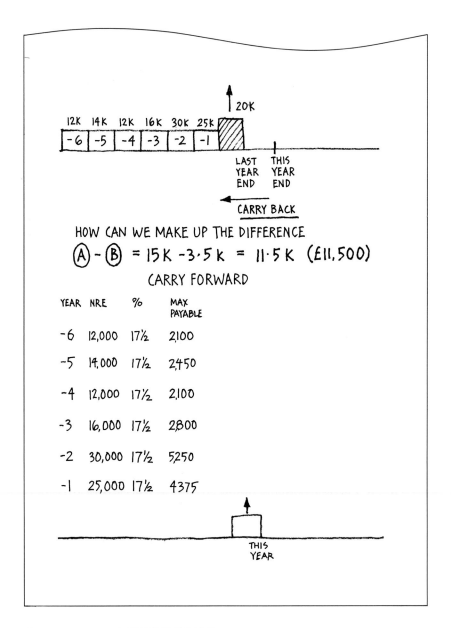

HOW CAN WE MAKE UP THE DIFFERENCE

$$\text{(A)} - \text{(B)} = 15K - 3\cdot5k = 11\cdot5K \quad (£11,500)$$

CARRY FORWARD

YEAR	NRE	%	MAX PAYABLE
-6	12,000	17½	2,100
-5	14,000	17½	2,450
-4	12,000	17½	2,100
-3	16,000	17½	2,800
-2	30,000	17½	5,250
-1	25,000	17½	4,375

the accountant is ESSENTIAL. I have relied on clients providing me with information before now, and it has cost a lot of administrative hassle where premiums have been paid but were not eligible for tax relief and then had to be reclaimed, which is a very difficult process which I will not go into it here. BE WARNED.

For employees obtain copies of their P.60 earnings record slips.

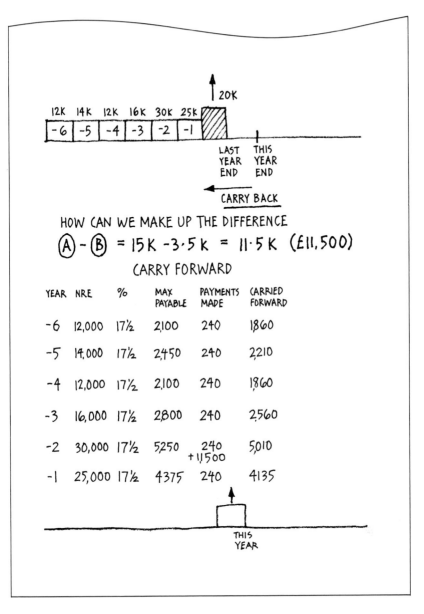

HOW CAN WE MAKE UP THE DIFFERENCE

$$\text{(A)} - \text{(B)} = 15K - 3.5k = 11.5K \;(\pounds 11,500)$$

CARRY FORWARD

YEAR	NRE	%	MAX PAYABLE	PAYMENTS MADE	CARRIED FORWARD
-6	12,000	17½	2,100	240	1,860
-5	14,000	17½	2,450	240	2,210
-4	12,000	17½	2,100	240	1,860
-3	16,000	17½	2,800	240	2,560
-2	30,000	17½	5,250	240 +11,500	5,010
-1	25,000	17½	4,375	240	4,135

For the purposes of this illustration I will assume that we do not know what the net relevant earnings actually were and this is just a conceptual presentation with our client pending a more detailed appraisal later on.

I then proceed.

Well let us assume then that we have earnings in these years [but not too outrageous].

"Can you tell me roughly how much you earned the year before last and the year before that?"

If they say "yes", we put their figures in. If they say "no" I say "let's guess" and that is precisely what I do and I write the numbers in above the boxes.

Now what we have to do is carry forward year "minus six" first.

Let's go back to year "minus six" and for the purposes of this illustration I am going to assume 17.5% for every year, [However, you will obviously look up the relevant figures for each year bearing in mind the person's age, eligibility and so on and legislation at the time and fill in the appropriate boxes]. then construct a matrix table underneath the words CARRY-FORWARD on my A4 sheet.

It is then a simple matter to calculate the maximum pension contribution payable to take off from that any payments that have already been made, and then have our CARRY-FORWARD column towards the right-hand side.

Don't forget if there are a number of percentages that are the same, then use your calculator with a constant to save time and effort.

If the percentage rate is 17.5% then merely plug in .175 to your calculator × × then put in 12,000 and = 2,100 and then you don't need to put the 17.5% in again, just put 14,000 = and you get 2,450 and so on down your table. 16,000 = 30,000 = 25,000 = .

If you are really smart, instead of pressing = you can press memory plus and it will store the running total in the memory for you so that when you press memory recall at the end of the list, it will give you the grand total of possible pension contributions. Also once you get used to where to put the decimal point you can just put in the 12, 14, 12, 16, 30 and 25 and move the decimal point to where you actually want it. However, I am aware that this is supposed to be a simple presentation and keep it simple I will.

We have now listed all of the carry-forward maximum pensions payable for our client. We now need to look at the amount of any payments made and take those off.

Well, just for fun, and to make the example look something like realistic, we will assume that he has had a £20 per month pension policy running for the whole of the last seven years. So again to put into our calculator 240, -, -, that sets it up as a constant and

we just have to put in the maximum payable in each time and that will give us our amount carried forward. Make sure, of course, you have cleared the calculator down before you start messing about with your new constant! Just put in 2100 = and we have 1860: 2450 press = 2210, 2100, 1860, 2800 = 2560 and so on down out list.

Again if you use the memory plus instead of the = then you will have a rolling total which will assist you in seeing when you have a full 11,500 which was the maximum gross pension premium that we could put in to get tax relief for last year, as an cumulative total on that carry-forward list.

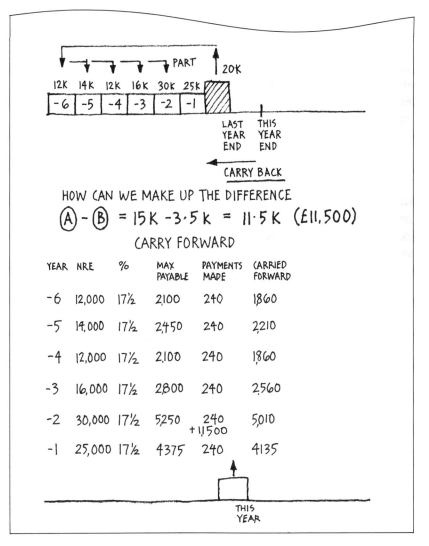

HOW CAN WE MAKE UP THE DIFFERENCE

$$Ⓐ - Ⓑ = 15K - 3.5K = 11.5K \ (£11,500)$$

CARRY FORWARD

YEAR	NRE	%	MAX PAYABLE	PAYMENTS MADE	CARRIED FORWARD
⁻6	12,000	17½	2,100	240	1,860
⁻5	14,000	17½	2,450	240	2,210
⁻4	12,000	17½	2,100	240	1,860
⁻3	16,000	17½	2,800	240	2,560
⁻2	30,000	17½	5,250	240 +1,1500	5,010
⁻1	25,000	17½	4,375	240	4,135

You could put the cumulative total just to the right of the carry-forward and from the A4 sheet, you will soon see that at year minus two you catch up to the £11,500 and in fact exceed it.

So I then put little arrows right the way back to year minus six over the top of the boxes and then bring forward little bent arrows and over year minus two I would put a bent arrow and PART.

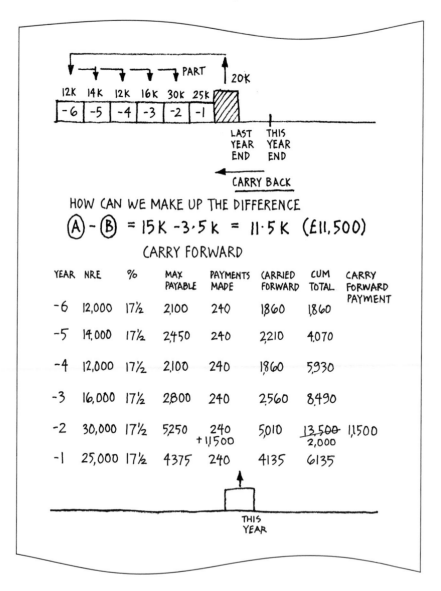

HOW CAN WE MAKE UP THE DIFFERENCE

$$\text{(A)} - \text{(B)} = 15K - 3.5K = 11.5K \; (£11,500)$$

CARRY FORWARD

YEAR	NRE	%	MAX PAYABLE	PAYMENTS MADE	CARRIED FORWARD	CUM TOTAL	CARRY FORWARD PAYMENT
-6	12,000	17½	2,100	240	1,860	1,860	
-5	14,000	17½	2,450	240	2,210	4,070	
-4	12,000	17½	2,100	240	1,860	5,930	
-3	16,000	17½	2,800	240	2,560	8,490	
-2	30,000	17½	5,250	240 +1,500	5,010	13,500 2,000	1,500
-1	25,000	17½	4,375	240	4,135	6,135	

Under the payments made I would put £11,500, I would put a crossed lined through the £13,500 that leaves £2,000 then add that to the next carry-forward item, which gives us £6,135 CUMULATIVE TOTAL to carry-forward to this year end. The process then starts again and this is the only occasion when I think one should use two separate A4 sheets of paper.

We are essentially going into a brand new presentation centred on this year end and the amount of pension premium that can be put away for this year.

There can be any number of reasons why people want to put a large lump sum into pension at a particular stage in their life, and that may be when **you** actually ENTER their life. They may be receiving a bonus payment, an inheritance or have just discovered they have a lot of money in the building society and have not been using it to the best advantage.

Moving into our current year, I again draw my line with this year end and the previous six years. We will look at the income for this year, if it is known or can be accurately assessed, look at net relevant earnings minus personal allowances, which gives us our maximum contribution for tax relief and calculate that out and then, of course, move to our net relevant earnings multiplied by the appropriate percentage rate for contributions in this year and establish that because, of course, that has to be used up first.

[A] minus [B] then gives us a figure in this instance of £15,950 which could be used in pension premium and attract tax relief.

Remember that year 'minus two' for last year end, now becomes year 'minus three' and we could feasibly start our table at that point as everything else has been used up. I show that graphically by merely scoring out the appropriate years with diagonal lines. Year 'minus three' would have part of it scored out because we still have some carry forward to use against this year end. The new table would therefore show carry-forward in year 'minus 3' of £2,000 the full amount for year minus two, less the £240 that I was actually paid at £20 per month and, of course, we have used all of last years up in our first exercise, therefore, there is no carry-forward left there.

We have £6,135 that we can set off against this year's tax, therefore, although we cannot eliminate the client's tax altogether this year, we have done a fairly good job for this particular tax payer.

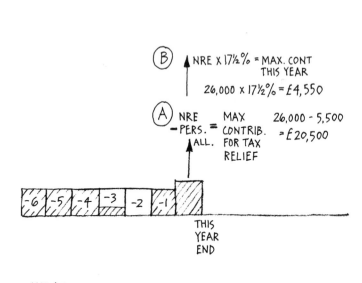

(B) ↑ NRE X 17½% = MAX. CONT
THIS YEAR

26,000 x 17½% = £4,550

(A) NRE — MAX 26,000 - 5,500
—PERS. = CONTRIB. = £20,500
↑ALL. FOR TAX
RELIEF

| -6 | -5 | -4 | -3 | -2 | -1 |

THIS
YEAR
END

HOW CAN WE MAKE UP THE DIFFERENCE?

(A) - (B) = 20.5k - 4.55k = 15.95k (£15,950)

CARRY FORWARD

YEAR	NRE	%	MAX PAYABLE	PAYMENTS MADE	CARRIED FORWARD	CUM TOTAL
-3	30,000	17½	5,250	3,250	2,000	
-2	25,000	17½	4,375	240	4,135	6,135
-1	20,000	17½	3,500	3,500	NIL	6,135

Case Study 1

Pat was an interesting client. She had been employed for eight years in a fairly senior position and had just inherited a whole bundle of shares from a doting aunt.

During the financial fact find, it was established that Pats main financial target was to have sufficient income to allow her to retire when the time came because she'd got a lot of plans, some of which entailed her going off to remote parts of the world, teaching english and seeing the local culture.

Although there was a company pension scheme, Pat had decided that she was not participating, having pointed out the error of her ways, we now had less than seven days to make the most of a good tax position for her before 'dropping' into a new tax year.

Again, the premiums weren't vast, but it was extremely useful to see how her objectives could be met and an instant growth achieved in her investment, just by using the 'carry forward', 'carry back'. By using the simple presentation, we showed Pat how to use up the existing tax year's £2,410. Then by going back into last tax year, 1988/89, having obtained her pay records, we were able to go back to 1982/83 and carry forward the amounts shown on the schedule below:

1982/83	£ 610
1983/84	£ 620
1984/85	£1,048
1985/86	£1,225
1986/87	£1,575
1987/88	£1,925
1988/89	£2,187
1989/90	£2,410

The total single premium capacity was £11,600 but of course because we were bringing this into a personal pension and Pat was employed, she only had to find £8,700 net to do the deal.

Pat was excited. She was going to make a positive gain on her investment at a twitch of a pen, but the money had to come from the sale of auntie's shares, so off she went to the Stock Brokers. The Stock Brokers allocated precisely £8,700's worth of shares to sell, net of their fees of course. The last settlement date in this tax year 1989/90 had already gone, Pat would not get her money until the next tax year started.

It is the first time I have ever organised an overdraft to pay a pension premium, but that's precisely what we did. The bank were assured by the Stock Brokers that £8,700 was on its way. Pat wrote her cheque. The application and the revenue forms 42 and 43 were made out and wizzo a 33% mark up in her actual investment, just by asking a simple question.

"Is there a company pension scheme"?

To which the answer is

"Yes"

and a second supplementary question which was,

"Are you a member of it"?

"No"

"Have you ever paid pensions?"

"No"

"Have you got a record of your earnings over the last eight years?"

"Yes, somewhere".

"Please find them. We can make your money make some money".

Needless to say Pat started a pension scheme on a regular basis from her income, but that's another case history.

Case History

Brian Ryder was a long standing friend, but some how we had never got round to doing business together.

Brian is sixty-four, well he was when we started working togetheer in 1990. Brian had been contributing regularly to a Barclays Life Unit Linked pension for a long number of years. He had been making regular contributions and also topping up with the occasional single premium. Barbara his wife worked with him as receptionist, message taker and general fact totem, and he paid her about £1,200 a year, because it seemed like a good idea. There was no real science to Brian's saving for pension, nor any real science to his overall financial planning for retirement for Barbara and himself as a couple. She was by now in her late fifties.

My first presentation was to Barbara and Brian and it was basically as shown in Wife's Pension. That saved Brian a lot of tax and established an income for Barbara in retirement to use up her personal allowance. (wife: Employee Pension Scheme).

The second presentation that I did concerned Brian's worries over a £2,800 tax bill that he was going to have to pay and that was going to deplete the £7,000 that he had got in the building society. Brian was not a tax payer, it was a club — he had written to them and told them — he did not want to join: but somehow.......

"Brian" I said, "why don't you retire?"

You know that glazed look that comes over people when they think that you have just made an improper suggestion. Well, Brian gave me one of those sort of looks.

"I can't afford to retire" he said, "where am I going to get my money from"?

"Besides that, I don't want to retire, I like my work" [Brian empties septic tanks and shifts "muck heaps"]

"No Brian", I said, "not retire, nominally retire"

"Is there a difference" he said.

Well, of course there is a difference, and I explained it to Brian.

"If we take the £7,000 from your building society [at this point Barbara had to restrain Brian] and put it into pension, that would wipe out your current tax liability of £2,800 - well all but, and then what we could do is see how much money there is in your pension scheme, retire you and then self fund your pension for when you actually do want to retire".

I got the glazed look again. With this case history it is probably best to set it out by means of a schedule, bearing in mind my A4 sheet principle and the fact that we want to understand what we are doing [and so did Brian].

Step 1. Take the £7,000 from the building society and put it into the existing Section 226 Barclays Life Pension Scheme [we had a reasonably up to date assessment of the fund, we knew how many units there were and confirmed that with the £7,000 added there would be about £25,000 in the pot]

Step 2. Contact Barclays Life and establish the Open Market

Option for the Fund and also the best terms that they were prepared to offer.

Step 3. Retire

Step 4. Uplift £6,894 and put that back in the building society.

Step 5. Tear up the tax bill [well not quite but confirm with the accountants the tax position for 1989/90 and the preceeding six years and get confirmation from them of the tax liability - then tear up the tax bill]

Step 6. Apply the £18,106 left in the open market option to purchase a pension for life in the sum of £2,443 per annum [annuity rates at the time were high and falling. [This was another reason for doing the exercise]

Step 7. Set up a new personal pension premium £2,400 per annum for the tax year 1991/92.

The SERPS Bus

23

CONTRACT JOURNEY TO RETIREMENT

Facets of the State Pension Scheme change from time to time and as pension specialists we are ask to comment and advise on what can be extremely complicated principles to people of whom it must be assumed "know nothing."

How would you cope with explaining to somebody the State Earnings Related Pensions Scheme from a Contracted In and Contracting Out standpoint?

Once again I feel that if the topic can be reduced to a presentation on one A4 sheet of paper, then the chances are that the general principles if not accepted straight away, are recallable in such a visual form that they will, over time, fall into place. The topic of pensions in itself is very "iffy" for people to understand. Beset with jargon and acronyms, coupled with self doubt and a possible mistrust, simplicity has to be the order of the day.

Remember the objective of this publication is not to say this is right and there is no other way, or even to discuss the principles of insurance, one product against another. The objective is to show how a complex subject can be put into one A4 sheet and perhaps to instil in you, the reader, the need to spend time to develop your own A4 sheet presentation such that you understand it and the person that you are showing it to understands it. Let us have a look at how I would explain the contracting out of SERPS.

"Everyone who pays full National Insurance contributions is entitled to the State basic pension", and I draw a box on the left hand side of my paper, about a third of the way down the page with the heading BASIC PENSION

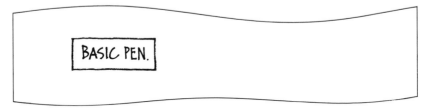

"Anyone earning over the lower earnings limit, which is set by the government with probable changes every year, will contribute to the State Earnings Related Pension Scheme. This is known as SERPS" I draw a second box attached to the top of the first box that I have drawn and I write in it SERPS saying as I do "State Earnings Related Pension Scheme."

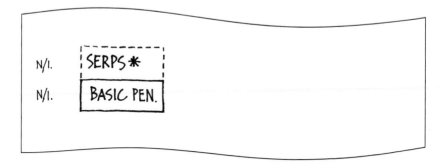

To the left of that I write 'N.I.' and '9%' and '10.45%'.

"Now of course if you are in the basic pension and you contribute to SERPS there is nothing to stop you taking out your own personal pension or joining a 'CONTRACTED IN' company pension scheme on your own account".

I draw another box towards the top of the page with 'PENSION' written in and 'CONTRACTED IN' as a title above that particular column.

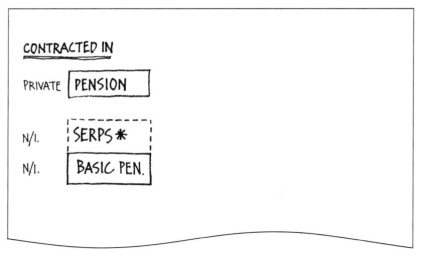

"Now I have said that we have a basic pension and we cannot get out of paying for that. It is an obligation which we have. Women used to be able to pay the lower rate stamp, but that facility is gradually being eroded away as they leave work, change jobs or whatever, so we will assume that everybody has to pay National Insurance contributions and here they have their basic pension."

"What you can do, however, is to opt out of SERPS [the State Earnings Related Pension Scheme] and we can effectively privatise that."

And here I draw a box on the righthand side level with my original basic box to the left and write in it 'BASIC' and then a plus sign goes above that.

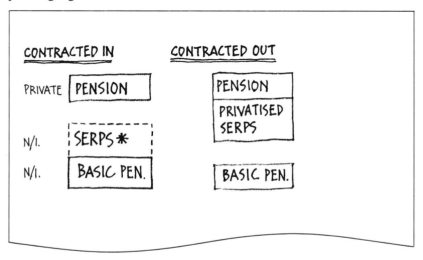

"We can privatise SERPS by giving the money to a bank, building society, insurance company, unit trust group, or whatever group is authorised to provide a 'protected rights' pension."

I draw another box and it says PRIVATISED SERPS.

"Just as before we were paying National Insurance to the government. What would happen here is if we 'contracted out' via a personal pension then the government would contribute to that by rebating part of the National Insurance contributions that we had already paid. If we had a 'contracted out' company pension scheme, then the company scheme could deduct the rebate from the National Insurance and pay that straight over to the insurance company or who ever and forward a lower amount of National Insurance to Department of Social Security."

"On top of all this, of course, we can do a 'personal pension' or a 'company pension' and contribute to it up to certain maximums.

So I draw another box attached to the privatised SERPS box which says PENSION in it' "and that is the general principle of 'contracting in' and 'contracting out' pensions."

I would have written to the right hand side of my right hand set if boxes N.I. - 2% employee; N.I. - 3.8% employer, Over L.E.L. [lower earnings limit]

You can see that it is quite easy to go on with this particular point to explain that over the years you build up a capital sum from which a pension is purchased to supplement the State Benefits. You can go into whatever guarantees there are and so on, again, in illustrative form, on the same A4 sheet using buckets, boxes or whatever takes your fancy to describe the fund and perhaps the surrounding Trust that protects the cash that has been built up. You can perhaps develop the presentation more when you move on to compare actually products such as Contracted In Money Purchase Schemes, Contracted Out Money Purchase Schemes, Personal Pensions and Fully Funded Pensions. The next chapter will give you an insight into that.

Case Study

In this case, a case study is not really relevant, well not in terms of one prospect, one company, one client, whichever way you want to put it.

In 1988 and 1989 I visited between seventy and eighty companies.

The odd thing about these companies was that none of the employers wanted to put in a pension scheme. None of them wanted to spend any money. Provided we could do the job for FREE , they would listen. Those were the terms that we were given in each case. We asked if we could talk to the employees, and the basic reply was

"not if you are going to create any hassle and get them all hyped up about a pension scheme, which we are not willing to put in if it increases the wage/salary overhead."

The one page presentation regarding contracting out and a companion one pager showing the benefits of a company pension scheme to the employees, at no cost to the employer, gained us thirty minutes to an hour and a half of the employer's time sometimes sponsored by the employer after hours with sandwiches, sometimes in the office, half employer, half employee time, but very few refused any time at all.

Therefore, the one page presentation [a] got their attention and [b] got us time in front of our clients, which were **the employees.**

The second thing is that the employees did not really want to spend any money. Lincolnshire is traditionally low paid, but not that low paid that they could not afford between £1.00 and £1.50 per week net cost to provide themselves with a

---

pension. That was our assumption and our starting point.

Before the first meeting with the employees, we had produced, from a list given to us by the employer, a simple one page presentation showing the employees earnings and the actual cost of contracting out. Using that and a flip chart, single page presentation, or an A4 pad where there were only two or three employees, proceeded to convert fifty-two of our seventy interviews into schemes.

I am not saying it earned us any money, but it certainly put the foundations of a good prospective future for all the participants into place.

We had already worked out that at the first renewal we would go back and do the same presentation again on the flip chart, but this time using a pre-prepared A4 sheet of paper with a triangle on it showing where the individual was today, what they would be earning when they were sixty-five, what pension they were currently going to purchase with their contributions, how much of their salary in percentage terms they were contributing, how much they should contribute if they wanted two-thirds final salary pension and we converted it all into today terms.

No telephone numbers. Everything that we presented related to today's values. In that way they could identify the State Benefits and add them on. (See Chapter 13)

All the had to do once we reached this point, was to determine whether they should contract out, through a Money Purchase Scheme, or a Personal Pension, and that is what the next chapter discusses.

Works Special

24

IN A BUNCH OR GOT IT ALONE?

Personal pensions compared to occupational pensions schemes.

"If we look at your earnings, year by year, we could represent that with a line on which I will put the Easter before last, last Easter, this Easter and next Easter."

I draw the line [as shown] and divide it roughly into four parts.

"You see in tax terms, years go by in terms of Easter eggs, rather than Christmas presents. So for these purposes just think Easter eggs. April 5th every year."

"Now from the Easter before last to last Easter let us assume that you were 'contracted in' to SERPS and then you bought a personal pension which enabled you to 'contract out'. Your National Insurance contributions paid by your employer would not have changed at all during that period, you would have received the policy document and the balance on the statement of accounts would read NIL.

"If we look at your earnings".

Here I draw a square umbrella over the tax year from the Easter before last, and the last Easter," then we would have been paying, as I say, through your employer, National Insurance contributions at the full rate to D.S.S."

I draw little arrows going up, twelve of them, if I am feeling really pedantic, going up to a box which says in it D.S.S. and N.I.

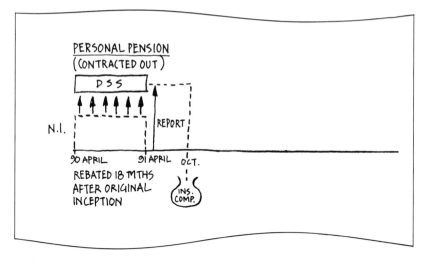

written at the side.

"Now last Easter your employer would have issued you with a P.60 showing your total earnings for the year and at around the same time, he would have calculated all of your earnings and sent off a form to D.S.S. [currently the P.14] to let D.S.S. know exactly what you have earned. They would feed all of that information into their computer and this would tell them how much rebate you were due. D.S.S. would then tie that up with the insurance company or other institution that you had taken your 'protected rights' pension with, [to enable you to contract out] and by about October of last year, they would have paid the amount due to the insurance company for deposit into your account. That is approximately eighteen months from the beginning of the tax year in which the National Insurance was actually paid."

Now let us say that last year you decided, in April, to join a company pension scheme.

You are not eligible to be a member of a personal pension scheme and an occupational pension scheme at the same time if you have only one source of income. The rules simply do not allow it. You would stop your 'protected rights' personal pension. That is no problem. D.S.S. would still pay the amount that was due to you [from the Easter before last to last Easter] into your account last October [are you still with me]".

"However, from April last year, your employer would actually deduct less National Insurance from you than had previously been the case. Once you contract out, you are entitled to the N.I. rebate

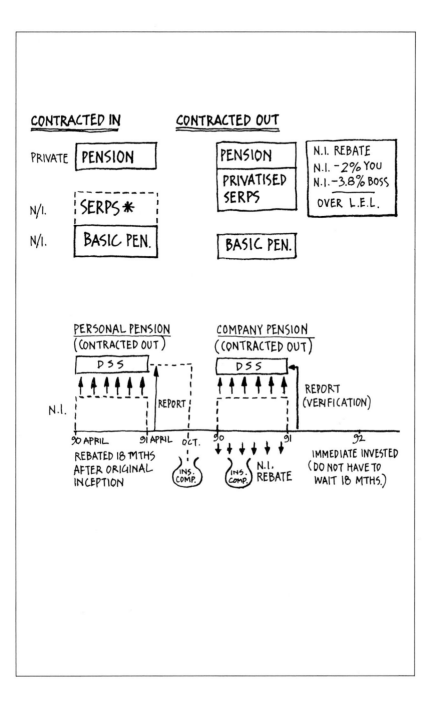

and as your employer has an 'occupational pension' scheme, he can actually pay those N.I. rebate contributions month by month direct to the insurance company on behalf of D.S.S. This does not apply to 'group personal pension schemes'.

"This means that your N.I. rebate is actually invested immediately, month by month, as it arises"

Here I draw shorter arrows going up to D.S.S. and some very short arrows coming down under the line, direct to the insurance company.

"You can see then that the only advantage, in purist terms, of becoming a member of a company pension scheme is the fact that your National Insurance rebate is actually allocated straight away by your employer. You do not have to wait for it. That investment timing can certainly produce a significant extra pension at aged sixty-five for the members of the scheme"

A lot of people would then beg the question

"But surely the personal pension can move from employer to employer far more easily than a company pension scheme?"

One could argue it either way. I prefer 'contracted out' money purchase pension schemes organised within the company for the benefit of the employees, therefore, how would I argue my particular corner?

Well, I have established that the National Insurance rebate is invested at an earlier date, therefore, the argument now has to hinge on portability.

"One cannot deny that a personal pension is yours, you may pay for it out of your own bank account. If you move from employer to employer, then you can take that personal pension with you. There is no disturbance to that unless, of course, your employer was contributing to your personal pension, in which case you will need to change the basis of paying contributions making sure that the employer cancels his direct debit, notify the insurance company, etc."

"Within the company pension scheme, you have, as I see it, a tray of beverages. Each person within the scheme has their own beverage, a cup if you will, on the tray. If Sue takes coffee without sugar, and Sally takes tea with sugar, and so on, then each person within the scheme can, as it were, select their beverage and how they like it.

You can do that with a personal pension, whether you contribute or the employer contributes, whether you have a unit linked or a with profits, or a mixture of both, is entirely down to you.

To a degree, that same beverage analogy applies to the contracted out money purchase scheme and the selection of how their particular beverage is mixed in terms of who contributes and how much. It is very much the same except that you do not have to bother your own bank to change direct debits. It can all be done through the company wages administrator and is done on a weekly basis, or monthly, as per your pay, under your direct control.

If you leave the company, then the company immediately stops paying in to the pension scheme. However, uplifting the benefits and taking it to another scheme in a money purchase environment is not an onerous task or as difficult as it used to be with funded pension schemes, where there were actuarial calculations involved.

The 'funded' schemes were a bit like a tea urn, where basically you have got whatever came out of the tap, and you really had to rely on whoever put the brew together as to whether it was palatable or not. The beverages on the tray at least allow you to see what your particular cup looks like and what the contents amounts to.

I firmly believe in terms of administration that there is little to chose between the schemes. However, time has shown that the D.S.S. have to be sure of their figures before they part with any money to protected rights schemes, and the time scale of eighteen months, from the beginning of the tax year, can extend considerably, whilst deliberations go on.''

This is not, however, the forum for great debates about which way the individual client should go against another.

The principle is the single page A4 presentation.

I then ask if there are any questions and refer back through my drawings to illustrate any answers.

Well you have seen the method that I have used to discuss and illustrate the difference between Contracted Out Money Purchase Schemes and a Personal Pension or Contracted In Money Purchase arangement plus Personal Pension arrangements.

What I feel that my job in front of the potential scheme members is, is to illustrate clearly and simply what they would gain and what they would lose. Most people seemed to understand the "tea urn" principle of the old funded schemes, which in no way detracts from those schemes if they are in place. The people that I was talking to had left those schemes and received, on occasions, "poor transfer" values in their eyes.

It could be that they had never been in pension schemes at all, but they had heard people, like their father, uncle, aunt or mother talk about the schemes in not too glowing terms. [Some of the old schemes did appear to be poor value for money, but only because the benefits matched up to contributions; which were derisory].

The "tray of beverages" concept helped people to understand that a Contracted Out Money Purchase scheme, which I personally favoured, was very similar to having a personal pension especially if they did not change investment managers when they changed employer.

However, I did explain to people "if you are <u>not</u> going to stay with this employer, don't join the scheme."

I work on the assumption that most people go to work for a company because they want to stay there, not because they want to leave. Remember the principle of this book is merely to describe simplified complex precepts. Whether you agree or disagree is irrelevant to the fact that the simplification of the argument actually worked for me and it can work for you, whichever part of the spectrum you feel fits the bill, provided you put your presentation together with a degree of thought- and lateral thinking.

As I said at the end of Chapter 17, this presentation resulted in fifty-two Contracted Out Money Purchase schemes being put into place and now, two or three years on, the employees are hiking up their annual contribution substantially.

This was from a position of ignorance, hostility and indifference.

Now they realise, because of the presentations that we have put forward, in today terms financially, that they need to put money away to be able to retire on a reasonable level of income.

The structure of schemes that we are talking about fluctuate from four employees through to thirty. It takes a lot of effort every year for us to produce our triangles and convert the insurance company figures into present day values. My company finds that it is worth it, and I hope that you will too.

Side Car Mole

25

SIDECAR SEMANTICS

Free Standing Additional Voluntary Contributions to pensions always present, in my experience, a conceptual problem. There is an old Yorkshire expression, "it's neither nowt nor summut" which about sums up the F.S.A.V.C. It follows none of the real conventional rules and yet it is such a simple contract that I am surprised more people do not make use of it.

The great down side that sales people put to me, and, therefore, must be putting to their clients, is that the Free Standing A.V.C. cannot be used for mortgages because there is no commutation value to draw cash. But there is you know, it depends upon how you look at it.

Do not confuse me with the facts, it is what I perceive that is the truth. Think laterally.

So how do I tackle the Free Standing A.V.C. with those that I deal with on an A4 sheet of paper and build in a mortgage repayment vehicle as well if that is what is required?

An area where I use Free Standing A.V.Cs might frequently be where the individual concerned is building up maximum benefits under a pension scheme.

"This is your pension at the moment"

and I draw the bucket. "Our problem is that funding for your normal retirement date, which within the company pension is age sixty-three, it is not possible to use additional voluntary contributions or extra company contributions to build up sufficient funds for say an early retirement at aged fifty-eight.

What we need to do is build up extra bemefits in a separate tank. Of course we still want to get the tax relief by treating that extra tank as a pension fund. The only way that we can do that satisfactorily is through a Free Standing A.V.C.

I now draw a second bucket at the bottom and to the right of the first bucket. I join the two with a "pipe."

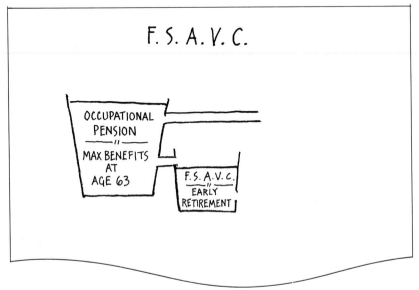

At the time of writing, £200 per month or £2,400 per year can be put into a Free Standing A.V.C without reference to the Pension Schemes Office, Occupational Pension Board, employer, Inland Revenue, Auntie Doris or anyone else.

"Technically, Mr Client, we are over funding your pension but, only to your current scheme pension age. You see for every five years that you retire early, you halve the pension benefits that you will get. That's a useful rule of thumb, although it is not absolutely accurate, it is as accurate as we need to be for this particular purpose."

The client may well ask "What happens if I do over fund?"

"The answer to that is quite simple, they will merely take the benefits that have accrued and pay you the whole excess lump sum back less a tax charge on those excess funds"

"The likelihood of over funding is very low. However, if you get exceptional returns on your investment, you may still be better off than from an alternative investment.

"What if I don't retire until normal retirement age?"

In that case you will, at least, have the maximum benefits for you, your wife and dependants, so who is really bothered anyway?"

Flippant? No not really. Practical.

I find people try and be too clinical, too accurate, too clever by half. " Life is a series of adjustments" - as John Savage, a well known Million Dollar Round Table speaker, says.

If my client does asks me what the down side is to a Free Standing A.V.C. then I tell him or her that it is the fact that a Free Standing A.V.C. has no cash commutation.

With most occupational pension schemes, where the cash commutation is rated as 1.5 times the final salary, the fact that a Free Standing A.V.C. has no cash commutation is irrelevant.

"What we do Mr Client is to pool the joint funds, the occupational pension scheme and the Free Standing A.V.C., and from this sum we create your pension." The cash commutation comes out of the total pool. The fact that the money actually comes from the occupational pension scheme and not from the Free Standing A.V.C. fund is, as I have said, irrelevant. It only becomes relevant if the 1.5 times final salary calculation amounts to more than is actually available within the occupational pension scheme fund. Again for the average person that will not be the case."

And so back to my A4 sheet of paper. I draw a box round the two buckets put an overflow pipe through the top to make up the tax

free cash sum, and stick a tap on the end of the Free Standing A.V.C. so that the pension flows through to give income.

I use a similar methodology to illustrate the use of a Free Standing A.V.C. for funding a mortgage. Where somebody isn't contributing for their full entitlement or perhaps they have got earnings [e.g. bonus, overtime etc] benefits in kind emoluments that are not taken into account in their occupational pension scheme, again I will use Free Standing A.V.Cs to pick up the extra contributions. Where I was limited in the previous example to the maximum non-certified Free Standing A.V.C, here we can use a Free Standing A.V.C. up to the appropriate maximum limits which may be 15% of income if the scheme is non-contributory.

A mortgage has to be paid off at some stage and an A.V.C. carries with it its own difficulties. It also makes the client's savings transparent to his employer. He may not want that transparency for any number of reasons, not least of which is that it undermines his bargaining position if there is a promotion going or he wants to negotiate a higher pay deal. The Free Standing A.V.C. is out of reach and, up to a point, out of sight of the employer.

There is no reason why an individual should not use a Free Standing A.V.C. to fund for a mortgage, as I say to the client during my presentation.

"Do not confuse me with the facts, it is what I perceive that is the truth." The perception is that we have an occupational pension fund which has a tax free cash facility and we have a Free standing A.V.C. which does not. That is the perception. The fact is that the tax free cash sum emanates from commutation of the pension fund. If we go back to my one page diagram I draw the occupational pension scheme bucket and I say to the client

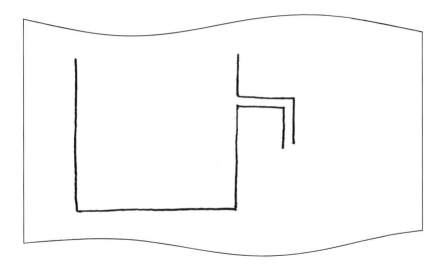

"We can set up your mortgage and what we will do is use your tax free cash sum at retirement to repay the mortgage. How does that sound?"

"That's fine" replies the client.

So I draw my bucket and I skim off the top of the fund like an overflow pipe to pay for the house. At this point, I remind the client, and you, that the reason the Government allowed 1.5 times final salary to be taken as tax free cash was to enable individuals to buy a retirement home, because, in the early days of pensions, many people were in tied accommodation. That hangover still subsists and I see nothing wrong in using this facility for that purpose.

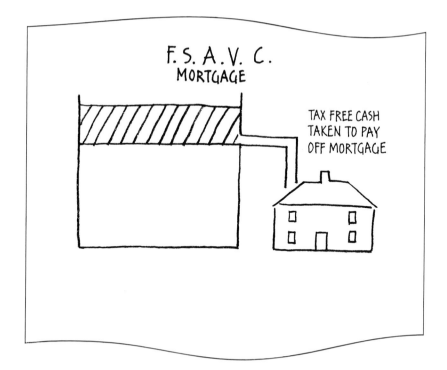

"Now the down side of taking that tax free cash to repay the mortgage on your house, Mrs Client, is that you will have a short fall in the income that would otherwise have been generated."

"You are not funded for full benefits under your pension scheme, you are entitled to twenty-five sixtieths when you retire. We are going to take 1.5 times final salary at that time because you will have completed more than twenty years service, but what about that short fall in income? As you can see we have taken a large slice of your income producing capital off the top of the bucket. For income purposes your bucket is going to look like this"

And I draw a second bucket towards the bottom of the page

"If we could top up our bucket to replace the lost income, would you want us to do that?"

Invariably people do not want to lose their retirement income, and the answer is

"Yes, please"

"Well, let us create a second bucket of money which is equivalent to the amount we have taken out in cash to pay for your 'retirement' home, that will produce income. You will receive full tax relief on the contributions at your highest rate of tax, and you will not lose

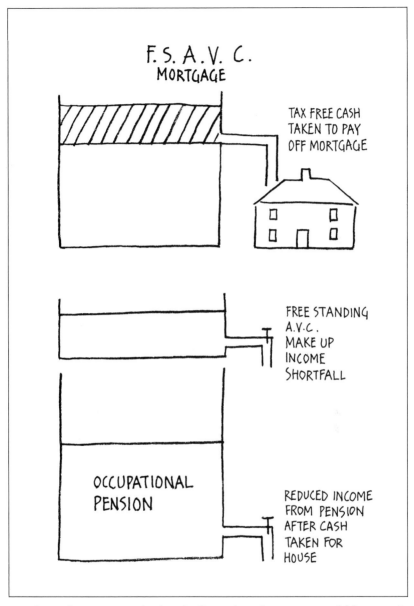

out, in real terms, on the level of pension that you would have got at age sixty when you retire — how does that sound?''

"Perfect.''

You see, all we have done is changed the perception. We have not taken capital to pay for the house. We have actually moved 'income' and 'converted' it to capital to repay the mortgage.

By that token we have got to replace income, not capital, at retirement. A Free Standing A.V.C. is perfectly designed for that particular task.

The other advantage of this, of course, is that whereas with personal pensions one is funding for mortgage with a total pension premium, of which only 25% of the fund can be uplifted to pay off the mortgage. With the Free Standing A.V.C. presentation, all that we are funding for is the lost income, in other words, the tax free cash sum pound for pound. It works out very efficient net of tax, when comparing it to an ordinary repayment mortgage. A Free Standing A.V.C. is a very useful tool and a simple change of perception can make it easily adaptable to an individual's requirement.

Case Study 1

This is an interesting case study because the subject is an ideal example of the type of individual who can assume, quite wrongly, that his pension is related to his total pay.

Our subject was a squadron leader in the Royal Air Force and he had just two and a half years service to do before attaining age fifty-five and bailing out. He was a pilot on a very good salary of £33,244.20 per annum. However, £6,559.05 of that total remuneration package was flying pay. His pension was based on the £26,685 balance, which was his basic emolument.

There are a considerable number of individuals that fall into this trap.

Ben wrote to me from his overseas posting in Italy saying that he had some money to invest. He had suddenly realised that he had to do something about advancing his income otherwise he was going to come out of the Royal Air Force and have to start "working for a living" all over again. He did not really want to do that.

Ben wanted to have enough income around him so that he could live in his converted cottage in Tuscany and take in bed and breakfast guests through the summer season to earn a bit of pin money and exercise his own, and his wife's culinary and hospitality skills. What could he do?

By using our simple A4 illustration, we were able to deal with this enquiry completely by post. The slogan "Buy Three

---

- get one free" also added a little flavour, which this particular gentleman understood and took to.

The result was that Ben was able to put £2,925 [£3,900 gross] into his Free Standing A.V.C. towards the end of the tax year 1990/91 and later pop another £1,406 [£1,895 gross] into a Free Standing A.V.C. in June of the 1991/92 tax year. Vertually as soon as it crossed the threshold of the insurance company, the investment had grown by 62%, because of the tax relief. Look at the illustration and see whether you would have jumped at this opportunity if you had been in his shoes.

Even with the policy administration charges and payment for our services, the return on capital is significant over a short duration. It improves over the longer investment period.

Case Study 2

AS few years ago we discovered a factory where a whole nightshift of fourteen people in the company pension scheme thought that they were contributing 5% of salary to their pension, [but I guess they had never actually checked the figures on their pay slip]. We checked, only to discover that they were actually contributing 2.5% of salary. Half of their earnings, yes HALF OF THEIR EARNINGS, were not pensionable. Remember "Do not confuse me with the facts, it is what I perceive that is the truth"

Well it was never any truer than it was with this band of intelligent, hard working, platers and welders. They had been on the permanent nightshift for three years when we came into contact with them.

Nobody had thought to talk to them about doing a Free Standing A.V.C. to pick up the extra pension that they would need in retirement to keep up their standard of living at the level of earnings that they had been used to.

They were earning more than their colleagues in other parts of the factory working a day shift, but proportionally they were not saving anywhere near as much as their work mates were. A simple presentation and over half of them made the necessary adjustments.

Squadron Leader Ben   17.08.35

Retirement age 56

Investment

Date	Gross Amount	Nett Contribution
21.02.91	£3,900.00	£2,925.00
06.91	£1,895.00	£1,406.25
	£5,795.00	£4,331.25

Top rate additional tax relief		£ 869.25
TOTAL NET CONTRIBUTION		£3,462.00

Benefit

01.09.91	"CASH POT" Uplift 61.6%	£5,620.30

Open Market Option (Scottish Amicable)   £ 706.68 p.a.

£58.89 per month for life

Mountain Top Mole

26

HOW IS YOUR MOUNTAIN?

How do you view your mountain? Your personal mountain. Do you see the summit bathed in sunlight, white clouds scudding over the peaks against the back-drop of a clear blue sky? Do hear the birds singing and the animal noises, the tinkling of bright fresh water streams?

Perhaps you feel the closeness and warmth of nature in the pine tracts that you walk through, the grassy glades, the sun bathed outcrops where you can rest and view the countryside.

Is your mountain in the lee of the wind, away from storms? Up hill but an easy path, or are you on the other side of the mountain?

The other side of the mountain has a sheer face of stark grey granite with rocky outcrops and a barren aspect. No sound of life. Just the chill murmur of a cold wind as it weaves its way between the dark outcrops. The only sound of water on this side of the mountain is from the rain or perhaps it is the soft rumble of snow as it crashes from the peak towards you as the avalanche gathers momentum. Do you feel fear? Panic? Or perhaps exhilaration at the challenge of this edifice which has to be conquered.

The odd thing is that both of these descriptions, the emotions, feelings and sounds, describe the same place, the same mountain, but from a different perspective.

The route that you take to the top depends upon your own

personality, your own drive, your perception of pleasure and of pain and in what you find exhilarating or stressful.

I think it was Larry Wilson, of 'Wilson Learning' at a Wembley convention, who first brought to my attention the phenomena of U-stress and D-stress and I can best amplify the principle by giving you an example and letting you feel the emotion yourself.

Visualise: You are in an aeroplane at 3,000 feet with a parachute on but you have never used a parachute before. At this point, I believe it would be correct to say that whoever you are, you are feeling "stress". Apprehension. The door has opened and you are ushered towards it and in the next seconds you are hurtling towards the ground, the only sounds that can be heard are the rushing of the wind past your body and the sound coming out of your mouth.

WAAAGH !! is D-stress.

This is the sound of a person who did not want to be there in the first place. It is every other persons fault that they are now falling through the air, they do not know if the parachute is going to open. When they get to the ground will it come up to meet them so fast that they will break every bone in their body? Is this you? Is this your average day?

or

WEEEEH!! U - Stress

What a feeling. I have never felt anything like this before. Hell, even if the parachute does not open I am enjoying myself. however, I know it will because I know the lady who packed it. Landing is no trouble. I have just got to make sure that I run with the wind and fall over as they taught me. Everything is going to be fine. This is U-stress

In both cases the adrenalin is flowing, exhilaration in a different form may be apparent, perspiration is exuding from every pore but the personal experience is of pleasure or pain....

So it is with our personal mountains. There can be so much that we want to learn, but we tie ourselves to somebody who gains pleasure from going up that stark foreboding face instead of taking the gentler route. Or perhaps we attack the Eiger or Himalayas before doing some simple hill climbing in the Dales.

My experiences over many years of life assurance and pension planning have taught me that there is as much pleasure and satisfaction in delivering cheques to families as there is in delivering cheques to corporations.

Providing a vital financial transfusion to those in need makes every mountain I have ever climbed worthwhile, and I hope that in these pages, as you emerge from your molehill, your mountains will be pleasurable, exhilarating and fulfilling whatever form they take.

Also published by WITHERBY

YOU SIGN
by Terence P O'Halloran   £7.95

CONTENTS

FROM THE FOREWORD

Terry O'Halloran has been long enough in the business, which is why "You Sign the Little Cheques and We Sign the Big One" sticks to basic principles but at the same time puts them across in simple terms. When I signed my first little cheque for £6 a month on my first life policy back in 1965, I was given a single sheet of paper with some figures on it which I didn't understand. Fortunately I lived long enough to enjoy the proceeds, with my family, of the big cheque for £8,944 which arrived in 1990.

Vincent Duggleby
Presenter: **B.B.C. 'Moneybox' Programme**

"We have a tremendous responsibility providing true life after death. Everyone else brings sympathy – a Life Assurance salesman brings money and with it hope for a future."

'You Sign' ...... has been the key to many sales for the novice and the experienced professional.

A simple INDEPENDENT guide for interview back up – 'You Sign' .... is a must. It sells insurance and makes sure that the client keeps it in force.